the
FLOURISH
FORMULA

the
FLOURISH
FORMULA

An Overachiever's Guide to
Slowing Down
and Accomplishing More

COURTNEY PINKERTON

BIRD IN HAND PRESS

BIRD IN HAND
PRESS

PO Box 1505
PMB 18545
Austin TX 78767

Published 2018
ISBN: 978-0-9994092-1-3
Edition 1 (Paperback)

Editing: Richard Amory
Cover Design: Rebecca Pollock
Author Photo: Margie Woods

To Judy Pinkerton

Thank you for pointing out the tiny flowers
as I raced up the path.
You were showing me a pace to live my life.
It turns out you were right.

CONTENTS

FOREWORD

If it were easy to change your life, there wouldn't be a million books about how and why to do it. I don't read those kinds of books but I've read and lived this one. Being married to someone who is in the business of personal transformation can be disruptive.

In the first half of 2017, Courtney wrote *The Flourish Formula* manuscript, I left the job to which I had dedicated myself for nine years, we sold our house and we sold or gave away everything that didn't fit into five suitcases and five carry-on bags. In late June, we flew one way from Dallas to Nicaragua.

The only constants were the five of us – we have three children, who were then six, eight and ten – and the business that Courtney had been nurturing for over five years. During those years, I had gone through something like the seven stages of grief in response to her explorations. It began with the decision to resign from her job and launch her own, brand new something (to be determined). We became a one-income family, which had never been the plan – we were both nonprofit types. I knew that she would create something interesting and valuable but assumed that it would take years for her to earn even part of a living.

Courtney built Bird in Handing Coaching out of the raw material of her own experience and with a massive appetite for learning. Early on, her investments in training and development far exceeded the revenue she generated. It only made sense and it drove me a little crazy. (Those *two* Harvard graduate degrees weren't enough?)

As the state of the business became a flashpoint in our marriage, especially at budget time, we learned to distance ourselves from the topic. I went from not understanding her process to being mostly unaware of it. As long as she was busy behind the office door or leading a retreat somewhere, my challenge was to have faith and a little patience.

Her writing of this book was a tipping point. Working on a very aggressive schedule, Courtney brought the energy and spontaneity of her weekly blog posts to a very different form. *The Flourish Formula* is an instruction manual and a manifesto. It's also a kind of memoir, which describes much of what frustrated and sometimes baffled me through her wilderness years of research and experimentation. When we finally agreed that it was time for me to read it, I saw a lot of our story on the page. I got it.

Perhaps not coincidentally, we decided at that point to change (almost) everything and move to Nicaragua. Why? Courtney and I met here as Peace Corps Volunteers in 2001. We worked together, fell in love and married here. Nicaragua is a special place, where we have done some of the hardest and most important learning of our lives.

In Dallas, we had become restless with our two-car, air-conditioned lifestyle. We had become acutely aware of how much energy, imagination and cash we spent on our mid-century suburban home and yard.

We wanted to put ourselves into an environment where we could simplify and figure out what we "need" and don't need as a family. We also wanted to offer our kids the opportunity to learn Spanish and respond to another culture. We wanted more green time for them. We were looking for adventure.

Now that Courtney had established a coaching practice and had managed to put her story and teaching into book form, it was much clearer where she was going. She could do her work from anywhere with reliable wi-fi. If it was somewhere where women might want to travel for retreats, even better.

It felt as if the book itself was daring us to take our dream seriously. By the time we arrived in Nicaragua, Courtney had asked me to consider editing it. I agreed and, at times, it felt like I was peeking at her diary. She isn't afraid to share her own raw, messy emotions because she offers simple and practical (but not always easy) ways to respond to all of them.

I don't read books like this but I have seen up close that the methods she describes really work. It has been very satisfying for me to help her wisdom shine through the text as clearly and as brightly as possible. It has helped me understand what was happening behind that office door all those years.

The Flourish Formula was written for women who want to be more in love with their work and their lives. If that's you, you may need the support of one or more people who care about you. If they're at all skeptical – and if they don't read books like this – ask them if they'd be willing to read an 800-word foreword...and have a little patience.

Richard Amory
Granada, Nicaragua
March 2018

1 INTRODUCTION

"What the world needs... is a recipe for marrying la dolce vita with the dynamism of the information age. The secret is balance: instead of doing everything faster, do everything at the right speed. Sometimes fast. Sometimes slow. Sometimes in between."
— Carl Honoré, *In Praise of Slowness*

Why I Wrote This Book

I went through a big professional rupture about seven years ago. At the time, I felt like I was standing in a huge gap between my life as it was and how I longed for it to be. I was fifteen pounds overweight (you know the baby weight that clings well past the nine-month mark) and I spent a huge amount of energy responding to our young children's needs and trying to keep our home tidy.

Most painfully, I had just resigned from what I thought was going to be my dream job with no real sense of next steps. Having earned two Harvard master's degrees, I imagined myself shooting like a firework into the sky, raining down amazing ideas and enjoying a life full of delightful colleagues and meaningful contributions. Instead, my work flame had flickered brightly and died.

When I look back at a photo from this season of my life, I barely recognize myself. The strain of three children under five and a nonprofit job with heavy leadership responsibilities left me depleted. Stress, like a layer of dust, had *seriously* diminished my sparkle.

This whole experience made me wonder who I was and what value I offered. My only strategy at the time was to come to a screeching halt. This was, honestly, pretty brutal. I felt a kind of psychic whiplash as all the forward momentum I had cultivated as a young woman deposited me in a very unsatisfying present.

How many "young women's leadership conferences" had I attended? How many hours had I studied social entrepreneurship, nonprofit management and social change movements? How many times had I won awards for being a "changemaker" or "innovative leader?" And what the hell was I doing now to make any kind of impact beyond attempting to care for my one, very troubled heart? This felt like a seriously underwhelming accomplishment.

I built my own library of personal growth books and spiritual memoirs and consumed them at a rapid clip. They would soothe and comfort me. I would recognize myself in the struggle of others and feel inspired; then I would put the books back on the shelf and be deposited back in my regular life. Day in and day out, I drank in coaching, meditation and other resources in an effort to find a path home. It felt very lonely.

While I had beautiful spiritual teachers who were lifelines through this process – one who introduced me to the Enneagram, an ancient personality map, and another who was an experienced life coach full of real world wisdom – they did not seem to speak the same language. One was gifted at the deep dive, the other the day-to-day steps forward.

I longed to know how to integrate them – how to take the shimmering spiritual truths and actually *live* them. I wanted to feel freer and more present. I absolutely wanted to stop feeling like I was missing my children's lives because of the pace of my work and internal pressures to contribute. I was tired of consuming myself on the inside to accomplish on the outside, even if my accomplishments were about service to others.

Though I didn't know it at the time, what I most wanted was for someone to hand me a magic elixir – a formula that would free me to both discover and release my unique gifts to the world *and* to flourish in my personal life.

I wrote this book to be such a formula. To show you exactly how to slow down and create more space for what you really want in your life. I suppose it's possible to sprint through life and be truly happy; but, in my experience, if we only have one speed, pressing us ever onward or even accelerating, it becomes impossible to notice the subtle course corrections we need to make along the way.

Full speed ahead sets us up for some unpleasant outcomes: a body breakdown – because all that stress wreaks havoc on your tissues – and/or a serious episode of work-related depression, in which you arrive breathless at the top of your particular mountain only to wonder, "What the hell comes next?"

I want to help you avoid this type of physical and psychological pain, but there's a deeper reason I want to share the Flourish Formula with you. I don't believe that you would be reading this book if you did not have something precious and potent to share with your community and our world – something unique and sorely needed.

Now is the time for well-resourced revolutionaries. We need women who are able to step in all our wholeness into leadership roles of every type, from our families and neighborhoods on up. When we are stuck in patterns of sprinting until we collapse, we never actually build the capacity to unlock and share our unique gifts.

Now, please don't hear this as further pressure. I am one hundred percent sure you are a superstar in many, many ways. You likely have excelled at school or work or both, you may be a charmer in front of a room, or a gifted writer, artist or entrepreneur. The last thing you need is to feel burdened by your talents.

But just as we can't nourish our bodies on fast food, we can't nourish our gifts living fast. Slowing down and establishing a more vibrant and sustainable pace allows us to discern what we uniquely have to share (thank God we don't really have to do everything) *and* to know ourselves well enough to craft lives that fit us completely. Not lives that others may expect or want for us but lives that make us tingle with delight. That is what is waiting for us on the other side of the Flourish Formula.

A Quick Tour of The Flourish Formula

So where exactly are we headed? In Chapter 2, I tell more of my story. In Chapter 3, I walk you through the framework of The Flourish Formula and talk about how to use this book and approach this process. But before we plunge in, I want to briefly share the eight steps.

F – Figure out the box you are in. The first step is to figure out the box you are in using the most incisive tool for self-awareness I have encountered: The Enneagram. In Chapter 4, you will discover whether you lead with your head, heart, or gut and will learn how to use this ancient personality tool to become more stress-hardy and resilient.

L – Learn to have a love affair with your work. In Chapter 5, we talk about your relationship to work and how you can transform it from a utilitarian exchange centered around a never-ending to-do list and instead build a more dynamic relationship, even a love affair.

O – Overcome your gremlins. The third step is super important – how to deal with those "gremlins," or the inner critical voices that inevitably appear when you start to make changes in your life. These voices actually become louder when we are growing! In Chapter 6, I share my favorite techniques for finding freedom from their influence.

U – Understand the language of your body. It is impossible to create real and lasting change or to contribute your own most potent gifts without finding a way to tune into your unique pattern of holding stress and the specific resources your body needs to thrive. Chapter 7 is where we learn to tune into those body-based signals, decode what they are telling us, and identify fresh strategies for nurturing your physical wellbeing.

R – Reset with meditation. In Chapter 8, I share a definition of meditation that I think will surprise you.

You'll discover a wide range of options that can help you detox your nervous system and find the right meditative practice for you in this season of your life.

I – Immerse yourself when stress builds. Chapter 9 is all about how to take care of yourself when the wheels come off. Consider it a menu of experiences to immerse yourself in the next time pressure is building and you are not sure where to look for relief. These nine centering practices also track with the nine Enneagram types so, based on your personality, there is one that will especially benefit you.

S – Schedule your Flourish Calendar. In Chapter 10, we bring the whole process together in a very concrete way by showing you how to create your own custom Flourish Calendar and a plan for how to live it.

I've devoted Chapter 11 to common obstacles so that you are prepared to face some of the challenges that may come when you decide to put this book into action.

The final chapter includes my dream and hope for you and suggestions for next steps. This includes a reminder to:

H – Hold it lightly. Any coaching or personal development book can end up feeling static or formulaic.

Step H is an invitation to make this process your own. It is also a reminder not to use these recommendations to beat yourself up or judge yourself harshly if you don't implement them perfectly. Such an all-or-nothing attitude doesn't serve you. It is a distraction that gets in the way of growth. Throughout the book, I will show you how to approach these shifts from a place of kindness toward yourself, which is a much more powerful way to create lasting change.

You Don't Have to Do This Alone

If any part of you feels demoralized – like you barely have the bandwidth to read this book without falling asleep and you can't imagine how you could possibly make the changes I will invite you to make – I want to offer some encouragement. I have been supporting women in unlocking their unique gifts and studying this relationship between our inner lives and our greatest contributions since 1999.

Many of the women I have worked with were navigating life challenges that may be different than yours. Some were leaving abusive partners to begin new lives with their children. Others were overcoming extreme poverty in rural Nicaragua to start a community bank. Yet each of the women with whom I have worked has always had her own inner mentor. No matter how challenging the externals and how loud the inner voices of doubt – and even if she chose not to risk it and go for the thing she desired – *she always knew what it was.*

That desire for a change – even something as simple as "I have got to slow down!" – is where all the good stuff begins. At this point, it is all we need to know.

I can say with total confidence that you can do this. But (and this is the really important part) you have a choice. Maybe you don't want to let yourself really imagine you could enjoy a more spacious schedule without sacrificing your ambition because of all the times you set that intention to slow down and didn't follow through. Or you tried again and again, without the hoped-for results. Or perhaps you prefer to stay a little bit dim and stress-dust-coated so that others can feel comfortable around you.

This is what I believe: This change you want to create – your new business or nonprofit venture, your best research or contribution to your field, your book or other creative project, your "I don't even know what to call it but I know I was made with it inside of me to share" – it comes from your essence, your deepest you. Even more than that, it is a gift from Source, God, the Universe. It is your spiritual inheritance. (Who knows how to wrap words around these things?)

This thing that's inside of you won't go anywhere. You can ignore it. Check Facebook. Watch Netflix. Pour another glass of Pinot. Distract yourself with drama of friends or family. Consume the news feed with no filters, no matter how toxic.

It will still be there. It is yours. And it is not yours. And it is ready to be set free. In fact, it is going to get more uncomfortable, fluttering its wings against your rib cage until you give it voice and release it to flight.

This is a crazy pants moment in history, so I'm doubling down on the truths and the work I hold most dear. Helping women unlock their gifts. Know that you don't have to do this alone. In fact, I don't think we *can* do this work alone. We get caught up in our own tight thoughts. We trip our own stress responses. It feels like our circuits are overloading, so we just stop.

The decision is yours to make. If you have been wanting to slow down but you haven't done it yet then ***you are getting more from not doing it than from doing it***. In fact, being overly busy can be your ally in never getting around to doing your most important work.

Maybe you want to keep it in the world of romance. "Someday..." Maybe it feels so tender and sacred you don't want it sullied up by the world and other peoples' opinions and judgments. Maybe you don't yet know how to grow into the person you need to be to create it. Or you simply lack clarity about how to go about doing what you desire or how to even know what your unique contribution may be.

There is another way – a way to create things out of your essence rather than your ego. It requires frequent immersions back in Source and constructing a firm scaffolding inside. This requires knowing and trusting yourself at a whole new level and, dear one, getting to be fully human. Not pushing the spiritual bypass button and pretending that life's challenges don't cut but instead living here and now in this one beautiful body, vulnerability and all. So that you can respond creatively, again and again, to life.

Why NOT to Read This Book

Before you say yes to this book, I have to tell you why not to read it. Please don't read this book if you think you have to already have it all figured out. Leave some room within the process for your beginner's mind. Also, please don't read on if you are not ready for action. We move through different phases of any growth or change process. Sometimes we are dissolving the old you. That is beautiful. Sometimes we are researching what could come next, which is also beautiful.

Then there comes a time to take steps. They may at first be extremely tiny steps (in fact they probably should be) but they build our capacities for discernment. They generate data for us to observe. "When I try this, that happens." And most of all, we learn. Not in an abstract way but in a full body experience of, "OK I'm going to own this and try it out and likely not get it right on the first pass but something interesting is going to happen." And at the other side of that is failure. Lots and lots of failure. Lots of busyness creeping back in. Lots of thoughts that won't let you meditate in peace. Lots of "This is harder than I thought," or "It isn't working."

Failure is part of the recalibration process. It is simply evidence that you have tried. The lessons you scrape off the forest floor of your heart may seem like muck but they're actually rich compost for the new life you are cultivating. Your dream will indeed take root, just not on the first pass. So please don't read on if you need instant success.

Yours For The Taking

Maybe, like me, you have one of those personalities that is never satisfied. You reach one plateau and pause briefly to catch your breath while looking further up the mountain. I don't know what change you will make but I know that it matters, that your voice and skills are here for a reason. We just need to crowd out those old habits of racing through life or hopping from goal to accomplishment so you have the bandwidth to create it.

Life is not only about being generative. It is also about receiving. In fact, not knowing how to receive is what blocks many women from truly sharing their gifts. As part of this Flourish process, I will teach you how to "go receptive" in a way that feels authentic to you. This enables you to fill back up easily when depleted and to operate from a solid core even as you reach and stretch. You will learn how to craft a custom formula of mind-body and meditation practices that make you feel supported in your own life. Practices that greet you in the morning and tuck you in at night and catch you when you are crashing and celebrate with you when you fly. We will build your resiliency.

There is nothing better than engaging in a love affair with the world by sharing your changemaking craft while taking good care of yourself. Ironically, slowing down opens you wide for success. Not just success "out there" but a full-on encounter with life in its crazy, throbbing beauty. A life lived at a pace that *feels good to be in,* full of presence to the people and the activities you find most precious. This is yours for the taking, for the savoring and for the receiving.

Are you in?

2 MY STORY

Rupture

About seven years ago, I was pushing my son Coleman on a swing in our front yard. It was an early fall day, which in Dallas means it was still quite warm. He was happy and in that tender phase of childhood where the fleshiness of the preschool years is melting into the leaner lines of elementary school. He was growing.

He was growing and I was miserable. I felt stunted and cramped and deeply unhappy, as well as surprised by how I ended up so cornered and squeezed in my own life. Only a few months earlier, my husband had discovered me weeping in our bedroom closet. I'm not sure why I chose the closet exactly, except that I felt my heart breaking and didn't want a witness.

Somehow the movement of pushing my son on the swing, the rattling of the leaves around us, the wind and the sun pierced my fog of indecision and I knew it was time to go – time to resign from my job, even though I felt so depleted I had no clue where I would turn next.

This isn't just a story about leaving a demanding nonprofit job so that I could be more present to my three young kids, even though that was how I thought about it at the time.

What I can see clearly now is that it was really a decision point about pacing. It was about the speed with which I was going to live my life. And it was about committing, even when I couldn't see the way forward professionally, to the belief that there had to be a way to design my life that broke through the fog of busyness. A life that invited me to be fully present to myself and my family *and* freed my most important gifts for the world.

I have spent the last several years discovering the tools and vital mindset shifts that make this transformation possible – how to design and relish an intentional and impactful life. This is the Flourish Formula.

Your Optimal Life Pace

Now, your story may not require such a dramatic shift in employment. Or it may. It's probably too early to know. As a coach, I have worked with hundreds of busy women, some of whom love their work and simply need to discover how to hold it differently so that it doesn't eat their lives. Others come to realize that the pace they long for is not possible in their current employment. They need support breaking down the big transition they want to make – to start their own business, change professions or simplify their housing or lifestyle – into clear, manageable steps.

Wherever you fall on this continuum, you will benefit from moving through the eight-step Flourish process. Because one thing I absolutely know to be true is that if we don't get really clear on the inner impulses that lead us to live life with such speed or internal pressure, we will simply recreate that pace in our new city / job / relationship.

While my experiment in slowing down felt more like being doused with icy water, I don't think it had to be that extreme or had to hurt as much as it did. But I had been numb to the gentler invitations to reevaluate my life – something I suspect you are more awake to or you would not be reading this book.

So before we go any further, I want to acknowledge one thing: It is tricky to talk about slowing down with you, my sweet overachiever. Because we know that anything, anything, ANYTHING can become a goal worth accomplishing and, conversely, fodder for evaluating yourself harshly and for failure.

This achievement/failure orientation doesn't serve us. It doesn't give us the room that we need to explore this important topic. Let me give you an example.

When I first arrived at Harvard Divinity School and Kennedy School, I was fresh off a volcano in Nicaragua where I had lived for two years in the Peace Corps. My time traipsing up and down Mount Tepezonat had been challenging. I even broke my ankle as a result of a nasty fall. But more than the terrain, what roughed me up were all the insecurities that those two years revealed inside of me. While committing to the Peace Corps allowed me to throw a meaty bone to my ego, which prioritizes *action* above all else – "Hey, look, I'm learning Spanish and creating great experiences for my grad school applications!" – what I was actually gifted in the day-to-day experience of working in my site was time. Lots and lots of time.

Sure, I was helping women organize development projects and community banks but that was, at most, one meeting a day. Add to that the trips to the well in the morning and afternoon and chatting with my neighbors and we are still only at about four or five hours. With no Internet, the rest of the time was mine to face. It gave me an opportunity to examine all of those inner demons that kept pushing me towards goals and accomplishments.

These years of service disentangled from our U.S. culture of speed required me to dig deeper within myself and to begin to discover tools that would support my ambition to "change the world" in a way that wouldn't consume me. Meditation was one of the tools I experimented with during this time and, honestly, it kind of saved my mental health.

But when I went to Harvard and my spacious schedule filled back up again, I stopped meditating as regularly and started feeling really smug about what little meditation I was doing. It moved from a soul practice to one held firmly by my ego. Because anything, anything, ANYTHING can be absorbed into a game of comparison or accomplishment / failure, i.e. dualistic thinking. In particular, I remember one afternoon sitting on the floor of the Cambridge apartment I shared with my brand-new husband (we met and married in the Peace Corps, he was a fellow volunteer) and meditating before I headed out for a meeting with a potential employer.

When I got to the meeting about the internship opportunity, I remember feeling super judgmental of this busy nonprofit leader who had made time to talk with me. I thought he seemed really distracted and not as present as I believed myself to be. I proceeded to rest in my enlightened judgment of him for the bulk of the conversation.

See how slippery this is? How even a practice as lovely and beneficial as meditation can become a measuring stick by which to judge yourself and others?

So please don't think that you should have already figured out how to make your greatest creative and professional contributions *and* enjoy a rich, spacious personal life. It is incredibly hard to create such integrated lives out of whole cloth. We have very few examples to learn from and fewer still who allow us behind the scenes of their process.

Likewise, please don't become a smug, "slow living" expert. Trust me, that is just an invitation for the universe to smack you in the ass. The Flourish process, like all the deepening experiences of life, is a practice. That means we have to practice it. And if anything in this book makes you think I have it all figured out in a permanent, never-struggle-again kind of way, please know that I certainly don't. (You can call up my husband and closest friends to learn the truth.)

What I *have* discovered on my journey and what I share in this book is how to slow down in a way that sticks – a step-by-step process that gives you the tools you need to discover and maintain a life that satisfies your ambition and feels good to be in.

The Productivity Trap

Before we dive into the tools and resources, let's acknowledge that this challenge doesn't always look as simple as just going too fast.

Sometimes, it is more a feeling of trying to do everything *all at the same time*. In perhaps the most extreme example of my tendency to try to do it all right now, my husband and I started our family when I was just half way through my dual master's program at Harvard. *On purpose.*

Then, because I'm nutty, we decided to try to get pregnant again in my final year and I was a couple of months shy of my due date when I walked. I got so winded during the graduation ceremony that some sweet classmates had to whisper up and down the line to procure me water and a snack. Their kindness in that moment has forever sewn them to my heart.

What about you? When have you tried to do everything all at the same time? What tends to happen to you when you do? I can say that my experience of squeezing in all the life I could hold did have some advantages. I was able to have my babies in my late twenties and early thirties when it was probably easier on my body. And my overwhelming need for help with a full grad school plate and a little one broke down my pride and impulse to do it all by myself, which led to some beautiful friendships.

So perhaps, like me, you have no regrets about some of these pressure-cooker phases of life. You are ambitious; you want to make a mark and show up and live fully. I get it. And there are seasons of life when this intensity is warranted. *But it is not sustainable.* If you live like it is, you will draw down your adrenal bank account and end up with both body and soul depleted. (Your adrenal glands are in your back near your kidneys and they play a vital role in producing hormones you need, especially in times of stress. You can also overtax your adrenals, in ways that have lasting, negative health effects, when you live in a constant state of stress. More on our fight / flight / freeze response in Chapter 7: Understand the Language of Your Body.)

This is a foundational lesson in the slow-living equation: *We are not made to be productive all of the time*.

We require phases of regeneration and renewal. If our pace cannot flex to accommodate these intrinsic needs, we suffer. Another challenge I encountered on my way to finding a pace that worked for me had less to do with trying to squeeze it all in and more to do with a funny way of holding time – as if my life was a resume and not a messy, dynamic unfolding.

Let me explain. I have a hunch that you have a plan for your life. An agenda. Goals that you stretch for. And as soon as you reach those goals, a batch of fresh goals emerges. You aren't motivated just by "the win." You're also motivated by a strong desire to be of service. You care deeply about our beautiful blue green planet and the people on it. You want to contribute in a way that is meaningful beyond your own small existence and goals help you take concrete steps in that direction.

I get it. I have also experienced the downside of goal-based living. Goals can pull us out of the present and out of the truth being dished up by our bodies and our senses. They can keep us pressing forward even when we need an adjustment. Goals keep us wanting to live towards the external impact or how we *think* it will look, over and above how we feel about it along the way.

So how did I end up crying in a closet and feeling so squeezed by my life I could barely breathe? It had a lot to do with the position I held as the leader of a small and very creative spiritual community. I felt deeply inspired by the people in this community and the opportunity to serve them. It was full of artists and musicians, nonprofit leaders, activists and academics. These people were changing things in our world for the better and I had the opportunity to help keep them refueled. I loved it!

Yet over time I lost myself in the work. I got a lot of attention for it. I was invited to speak at conferences and to share the stage with well-known thought leaders like Richard Rohr and Phyliss Tickle. Ultimately I became so attached to the *idea* of myself in this role that I underestimated the very real challenges it presented and failed to attend to the cues that were unfolding in the present, all around me. I also wrongly assumed that it would be a great job to have while raising three small children.

Time to Change

As the stress of my job heated up, I just kept on giving. I poured myself into it and would have continued giving all my time and energy in an effort to make it work, even if it meant consuming my own inner resources faster than I was replenishing them. Then came that fall day when, while pushing Coleman on the swing, I realized that I could not do that *and* have enough juice to be the person I wanted to be for my kids. They saved me from myself.

I decided that for the sake of my quality of life I needed to resign. I had no idea what I was going to do next. I just knew that I had to stop.

While this was wildly out of character (I much prefer to leap, or at least appear to leap effortlessly from one successful work venture to another, like a frog on a lily pad, thank you very much), I did stop. I took several months to heal, listen and learn. I did the things that I couldn't stop doing, like caring for my kids and basic household tasks. But otherwise, I just went receptive.

I gobbled up the Enneagram and other reading. I drank in several online training sessions and met with a coach. (A lovely colleague connected us by inviting me on an all-expenses-paid retreat. Otherwise, I doubt I would have even gotten started with coaching in the first place.) I read. I walked and took baths. But mostly, I just let myself dissolve the person I thought I was. (Having some savings was hugely helpful here, as we relied on that resource as well.)

I also rediscovered the simple pleasures that authentically fed me. Making art. Nature. Friends. I remembered who I was when I wasn't doing anything for the external validation. When I had no one inviting me to speak at conferences and no one following my blog. I didn't have a blog.

It was a rough time, I won't lie. I think it was much harder than it had to be, largely because I had little idea of what was happening to me. Now I know that it was just a normal part of the change cycle, or the process of human metamorphosis. (Martha Beck writes powerfully about the Change Cycle in her book *Finding Your Own North Star*.)

The first part of any serious change in life is akin to a death or rebirth. Dying to who we thought we were or how we thought it was going to go and the ego cracking open to make more room for the soul. When it was happening to me, though, it felt like I might never return from wherever I had gone.

And then, something shifted. I started having dreams of a different future for myself. Dreams of taking my spiritual teacher/leader impulses in a new direction as a coach. Ideas about traveling and working with other women who needed to slow down to deepen their impact. Suddenly, new resources appeared on my radar screen, like an online program for women entrepreneurs. (I had lots of awkward thinking about money and marketing to burn off on my way to soulful entrepreneurship.)

These shifts ultimately led me to study as a holistic life coach and create Bird in Hand Coaching. The meaning behind the name for my business starts with a thrift store find. I had picked up a fun vintage sign that says "Bird in Hand Tavern" at a nearby secondhand store. I loved it but could never find the right space for it in my home. One day, I realized that it was the name for my new venture! I love the resonance with the phrase "a bird in the hand is worth two in the bush." As a culture, we are often chasing the next thing when valuing what we already have is actually the more potent medicine.

It is my hope that all of my work – coaching, retreats, eCourses and now this book – creates gathering places, or watering holes for our more soulful sides. Parker Palmer is one of my favorite authors. He teaches us that the soul is like a wild animal and if we go racing through the forest of our own lives, we scare it away. So let's not do that, okay?

Instead, remember that your work is dynamic. And your life is not a resume. If you hold onto things in an abstract way, like checking boxes next to goals without staying attuned to the day-by-day unfolding and how you feel in it, you almost guarantee a frenetic pace and a less than satisfying experience of your one wild and precious life.

What can it look like instead? A few weeks ago, I was talking with a client who recently completed a coaching program with me. It was so wonderful to hear how she is flourishing in this new year: she is meditating, writing and reading daily, winning awards at work, and enjoying exercise and new bed time rituals with her little one, which give them both more rest and more time to dream. This is it. These are the moments that bring me such joy as a coach – not her "success" on the outside but the way her life feels delicious to her on the inside. She has created her own unique formula for living the life called out of her.

Let's help you create yours.

3 THE FLOURISH FORMULA

Before we begin to explore how you can slow down in a way that releases your most potent gifts, I want to start by honoring the passion that fuels you in the first place! I celebrate the deep desire you have to contribute with a capital C and I am absolutely certain that our world needs what you have to give.

But here is the thing: We gain nothing if we lose our quality of life for the sake of our ambition, even if our ambition is about serving others.

It is my deep hope that you will absorb the practices I have to share and make them your own. Not that they land in your head, but that you integrate them into real life where they can help you dissolve your old habits of pushing, racing and striving. Not because you *should* but because you want to find your way home – the place from where you can best share what you have with the world.

How to Approach this Book

The most straightforward way to use this material is to read the entire book and then go back to the suggested exercises in the areas that interest you. However, you may at times feel motivated to try out a new practice as soon as you encounter it, even if you don't yet know how it fits into the bigger picture. If so, consider yourself warmly invited to choose your own adventure. Pause to put down the book and experiment with a new practice in the moment. Or skip ahead to read chapters out of order based on where you feel drawn. I end this chapter with additional suggestions for integrating this material into real life, like how to design your own personal retreat.

However you read and learn, I hope that you will listen for moments when you experience a "ping" of recognition, when something rings true not only to your mind/ego, but also to your deepest self. But even as you read generously, I invite you to read critically. I joke about having an "inner Harvard" who believes in hard work and feet-on-the-ground thinking and an "inner fairy" who loves pixie dust and synchronicity. The two often duel it out.

When we are talking about things as effervescent and as important as designing a life that fits you from the inside out, we are always at the edge of what we can wrap words around. So please don't be afraid to wrestle with what you read here, push back, discern for yourself and test with your own experience. How will you know if you have found your truth to live? It always tastes like freedom. (This is an adaptation of a beautiful phrase attributed to Siddhartha Gautama, or The Buddha, who reminded his students that just as we know the ocean because it tastes of salt, we recognize truth because it tastes like freedom.)

This book is crafted as a series of steps. Each one is a "golden thread"– something to hold onto that pulls you out of the busyness fog into deeper alignment with your authentic or essential self – and they build on one another. But I also encourage you to navigate your way through the book according to the topics and areas that resonate most deeply for you. If there is one that you particularly resist, you might want to spend some time there, as well.

Trust that you will get what you need out of it and know that you are not crazy, you're simply growing! You're growing out of boxes that others might have put you in and you're growing out of your own box. You do not have to do this inner work and exploration alone.

Your Ideal Day

There is one simple practice I would like you to do before we learn more about the eight steps. (It is a variation on the Ideal Day exercise which is taught as part of the Martha Beck Coach Training Program and informed by Danielle Laporte's *Desire Map*.)

Take a few breaths, close your eyes, and imagine yourself at some point in the future (from a few months to a few years). Imagine that you wake up in your ideal day. This is not a day on vacation. It is a regular day, the difference being that it is structured in an optimal way. You have the perfect amount of rest and time to move between your various home and work activities. Imagine flowing through your day at a pace that fills you with gratitude and meaningful connections with the people you love and with the work you are called to create. Move slowly, taking in the textures of the day with all your senses.

How do you enjoy waking up and starting your day? Where do you enjoy breakfast? Outside with the birds? Coffee in your favorite chair with a few moments to journal? Continue moving through and keep exploring the day as it unfolds. Pay special attention to those transition points in your day or the "hinges" in your schedule that may currently feel squeezed or cramped.

For example, how would it feel to drive at a leisurely pace to school and to be one of the first moms to pick up your child (rather than the last)? Or to arrive home after your 9-5 workday to a fridge full of farmer's market goodies that you picked up over the weekend and have time to enjoy a new recipe? As you envision this day in your mind's eye, I want you to see if you can identify *how you are feeling in your body and emotions.* Is there one word that best captures it? Maybe you feel peaceful, satisfied or rooted. Maybe you feel effervescent, joyful, integrated, lit up by life. Continue with this exercise until you can identify one simple word or phrase. Trust what bubbles up for you. You can come back to this practice at any time.

Once you have your word or phrase, I want you to write it on a sticky note and keep it in your desk drawer. You may want another note on a day planner or journal or wherever you need the reminder. We will know we have created the perfect Flourish Formula for you not by how everything looks on the outside but by how it makes you *feel.*

The Flourish Formula is a step-by-step process for slowing down your life and upping your impact. It is what helps you unhook from praise and other external motivators to drop into a life that feels good to be in and releases your most potent contributions to the world. The Flourish Formula also equips you with tools that can help you find your way home whenever you start to feel scattered or overwhelmed.

Let's review the eight steps:

F – Figure out the Box You Are In. This is the foundation of our work together. Without knowing those inner marching orders that keep pressing you forward at an unsustainable pace, we cannot begin to form new habits. The Enneagram, an ancient personality map, is the most incisive tool I have discovered for getting clear on your core motivations and most frequent stumbling blocks. There are nine distinct personalities, three of which lead with their head center of intelligence, three which lead with their hearts and three which lead with their gut or body intuition. The Enneagram doesn't put you in a box. It shows you the box that you are already in.

L – Learn to Have a Love Affair with Your Work. What if your relationship with work was more like a passionate love affair rather than an exhausting to-do list that never seems to shrink? In this step, we are going to learn how to handle work envy (when you find yourself perennially feeling small in the face of others' accomplishments), make space for new priorities and allow what Martha Beck calls your "original medicine," that unique mojo you are here to share, to emerge.

O – Overcome Your Gremlins. Our inner critical voices or "gremlins" get louder when we are growing. This is very important to realize, since it will help you avoid the mistake many women make when leaning into new habits (like slowing down) or navigating growth opportunities and challenges. Rather than internalizing the gremlin voices and assuming that the inner criticism means "It wasn't meant to be" or that you are headed in the wrong direction, you will learn how to dissolve painful or limiting thoughts and to resource yourself as you move through them.

U – Understand the Language of Your Body. As an ambitious changemaker, maybe you are afraid of getting sick at an inopportune moment. Or you find yourself continuously crashing once the big project or event is done. Maybe you feel depleted and frustrated by your body breakdowns, which keep you from reaching your goals or moving at the pace that you desire.

In this chapter, we are going to identify several easy, DIY methods for keeping the stress in your life and body at a manageable level, as well as a few practical tips and resources for becoming the CEO of your own wellbeing (and who to recruit to be on your team). You have to be able to count on your body to support you in accomplishing what you are here to do and you need energy and resiliency to thrive in all aspects of your life.

R – Reset with Meditation. This step offers several easy meditation techniques that you can use to reset whenever the pressure builds. Unable to quiet your mind? You have come to the right place! In this chapter, I unpack some of the most common roadblocks to starting your own meditation practice and introduce a range of meditation options to help you discover one that fits you perfectly in this season of your life.

I – Immerse Yourself When Stress Builds. This step gives you a moment to catch your breath. It is not about introducing a new tool. It is an invitation to resource yourself with a fresh practice the next time you can't sleep or shut off the hamster wheel in your mind. (Remember step O? Those gremlins get louder when you are growing.) In this chapter, I describe nine centering practices, each of which corresponds with the Enneagram personality of the same number and has been designed to unravel some of the constriction felt by that particular type. However, all of these practices are helpful for anyone to use at any time.

While we all have one home base of our personality type, we also experience the whole range of emotions and human struggles. Think of these practices like a menu you can choose from the next time nothing else seems to be working.

S – Schedule Your Flourish Calendar. This is where we bring it all together. The Flourish Calendar is a foundational step to implementing the Flourish Formula in your own life. Imagine waking up feeling present, calm and at peace – and moving through your day with confidence that you are focusing on the right things at the right times instead of feeling guilty or distracted.

This step is your opportunity to customize a life and schedule that support *you* rather than the other way around. To do this we need elegant scaffolding: a greenhouse for those tender and beautiful shoots that want to grow in your personal, creative and work lives. This is how we nurture and ultimately share your greatest contributions: The Flourish Calendar. I'll show you step-by-step how to create your own custom Flourish Calendar in as few as twenty minutes. This is consistently one of my clients' favorite coaching tools.

H – Hold it Lightly. This step is simply a reminder that the way we hold these tools or practices is as important as what we do. If we make living slow or meditating another metric for evaluating ourselves (and setting ourselves up for failure), we end up adding stress rather than removing it. Hold it lightly reminds you that resiliency lies not in getting it perfect but in your willingness to try and to begin again.

How to Get the Results You Desire

Before we launch into Step F, I want to share a few tips on how to extract the most from your time with this book. I know from personal experience that if you simply read it and put it on the shelf or worse yet, if you leave it on your bedside table and feel guilty about not implementing the practices, you won't get the results you desire. These eight steps don't necessarily require a lot of time in your busy schedule but they do require *intentionality*. They require a commitment to tuning in to that slower frequency you already have inside and from which you can pick up your clearest signals for creating a life and work you love.

What does this mean? Consider how you like to learn something new or approach a big project. Do you tend to hole up and brew a pot of coffee and knock it out in one go no matter how long it takes? Or are you someone who prefers to take small, discrete steps each and every day? Honor how you like to learn and that will assist you in moving these practices off the page and into your real life.

If, for example, you like to tackle big projects all at once, perhaps you want to take this book, a notebook or journal and your laptop or phone (whatever you use for your calendar) and head off to a retreat house. Find one on Airbnb or a nearby boutique hotel for a night or two to yourself. If you can do it right now, wonderful! Or schedule a Flourish retreat for yourself sometime in the next month or so, over a weekend or any other day off. (If you wait much longer the trail will get cold and it will be hard to build on the momentum you create reading the book.)

I love to work in this way and the fresh-start feeling it gives me. Consider bringing some favorite food. Stop by a natural grocery store on the way to grab some easy-to-prepare meals: maybe a carton of freshly made vegetarian chili or sushi for dinner plus some delicious berries, easy to snack on baby peppers, even an avocado if you want to whip up some guacamole to dip your peppers in. (It's great brain food!) Whole fat yogurt, nuts, you know what you like, just make it easy and nourishing. And don't forget about the drinks: sparkling water with lime, a favorite kind of tea, kombucha. I wouldn't suggest wine while you are working through the steps just because we want you really clear and clean, in touch with what my friend and fellow writer Sarah Moore calls your "singing bowl self." But wine or champagne to celebrate once you are done for the day or at the end of your retreat would be lovely!

Bring your yoga mat and cozy clothes. In addition to making the process more fun it is going to help you move through the exercises from a place of lightness and joy. Feel free to take a big nap before you do anything else when you first get there. Then enjoy some focused time to hold your life and schedule in a new way. You can even make this a seasonal practice, marking off one night every few months to head off to a retreat and check in on your Flourish goals.

If a retreat is either not your preferred way to work or not humanly possible right now, there is another approach that can be just as effective: weaving dedicated Flourish time into your regular daily or weekly routine. Perhaps you want to close the office door, light a candle, set the timer on your phone for thirty minutes and work through these practices on your lunch break a few times a week.

Or grab your journal and a cup of coffee and move through them at the kitchen table before your household wakes up. (I've honestly never been able to peel myself out of bed early to do anything remotely close to "optional", so this choice would not work well for me, but I know it does for some women. I can appreciate how amazing it would be to feel like you have taken care of yourself *first*, before clients, children, fur babies, whomever.) Or maybe you want to spend a couple of hours every Saturday or Sunday morning after your yoga class. If there is another natural "slow down" time in your weekly schedule, that is a wonderful place to engage in some of these deepening exercises.

These are not either/or options. In fact, the most delicious way to integrate these practices into your regular life is to do both. However you approach it, all in one burst or bite by bite, I do invite you to make yourself a date or several dates to be with your most spacious self and these Flourish exercises and *put them on the calendar*. I offer a fun solo retreat planning and packing guide as part of a wealth of free tools for readers in my Flourish Kit at www.courtneypinkerton.com/flourishkit.

4 FIGURE OUT THE BOX YOU ARE IN

When I was a teenager, I used to really resent those Cosmo quizzes that would tell you your innate style. The questions always felt so formulaic and I struggled to answer them accurately. This weekend would I rather A) head out into nature in cutoffs, hair tousled and no makeup or B) get dressed up and go out with the ladies? Um – both please!?

As a girl, I had a love of fancy and sparkly things. Then, as I hit my Women's Studies phase at eighteen, I cut my hair super short and dyed it red. The night of my wedding in Nicaragua, I had to send friends out to get more razors so I could finish shaving my legs and don my handmade wedding dress. After two years of living on a volcano, I had gone pretty natural.

The point of all this oversharing? Those boxes – nature girl, fancy girl – they don't give me the space to live my right life, which includes both. Only now, as I land in my forties, do I feel the integration of these pieces. My love of a stylish pair of boots and a good haircut can coexist with my appreciation of the outdoors. Red nail polish can go with an afternoon gardening. I don't have to choose. The spiritual masters call this frame of mind "non-dual seeing." It is about learning to see beyond and around that very human impulse to put things in either/or boxes. It is not so much blowing the boxes up as dissolving them into a greater force field – or realizing they were never really there.

I've been alert to this dissolving of dualism over the past few weeks, as I have been in my creativity cave writing this book. I've always struggled with feeling a certain heat and ambition internally, a desire to make a mark, to make the world better in some concrete and demonstrable way (perhaps you can relate?). Yet, the rub comes from the fact that my nervous system is pretty sensitive. I have the opposite of what you would call thick skin. Plus, I'm a serious introvert. An INFP on the Myers-Briggs Scale. A dreamer.

So how to create the impact I crave? Clearly, networking events are out of the question as they make me want to vomit. It turns out that writing a book is a wonderful way for me to live into my own desire, to be of service and to do it from the comfort of my very own home! I don't have to pretend to be any different than I am. I can be both ambitious and introverted. Leader and gentle. Doer and dreamer.

I wonder what box you have yourself in. Would you like to dissolve it so that you can be more of your spacious self? Maybe for you, it is not about becoming a fancy nature woman or an ambitious introvert. You might feel stuck in different boxes: wanting to be both a present mom and a successful entrepreneur, for example, or an expressive creative and primary earner for your family.

Maybe you are passionate about a cause but want to find a way to not lose your entire life protecting the oceans or helping homeless women. Or maybe you feel stuck in the job and the life you *thought* you wanted when you were an overachieving twenty-two-year-old with little room in the box for those authentic desires that whisper to you now.

If so, please consider this chapter on the Enneagram your invitation out of the box you are in.

Why the Enneagram?

Compared to most personality typing tools, which can feel static or simply descriptive, the Enneagram is *dynamic*. There are nine different types or human archetypes. Identifying your type shows you that you are more than you thought you were and opens a wide path to learning and growing.

Once you understand that there is a difference between your personality habits (which you share with millions of people of your type from around the world), and your essence (which is one hundred percent, uniquely you) you can draw from the Enneagram to create custom "fieldwork" practices that help you in concrete, everyday ways to feel more at home within yourself, more able to reset when you get knocked down and, ultimately, clearer about your work in the world. I don't mean just your job or "what you do" but also your unique value.

Now, what does this have to do with slowing down? If our personality is in the driver's seat, we tend to speed through life or otherwise go on autopilot. There is another way. I'm going to show you how.

Olivia's Story

My client Olivia leads with Type Six on the Enneagram. I try not to say I "am" a type Three or someone else "is" a type Six because truthfully, we are so much more than our personalities. Instead, I say we "lead with" a certain type. Olivia's personality focuses her on living up to an internalized standard for what is appropriate or what a good person "should" do. Sixes are also busy "head" types, with anxiety just below the surface. They are very dutiful to the needs of others.

Olivia is a biomedical researcher at the Centers for Disease Control in Atlanta. She is in her midcareer and is very accomplished in her field. She recently applied for an elite award given by her research society. In the application process, she learned that a friend of hers was also applying and he asked for her help.

Now she was in a tight place. Should she support her friend simply because it's the right thing to do? Should his more senior status give his application priority over hers? How would her support for his application affect her own process? Her mind was racing, looping around and around the various options, unable to land anywhere that felt good. Together, Olivia and I talked about how her Six type operates in this "should" economy and I invited her instead to drop into her own heart and body and discern what she herself desired. This helped Olivia realize that she genuinely wanted both to help her friend *and* to turn in the strongest application she could for herself. The two impulses were not mutually exclusive.

She was able to respond to the opportunity from a totally different position: not out of duty or obligation but as a clean choice. The Enneagram helped her find her own sweet spot. Olivia reported feeling really solid and generous inside as she aided her friend and she followed through with her own priorities and ensured that she had ample time in her schedule to nurture her own application. Interestingly, this process also helped her to be more assertive and clear about her own qualifications, which came through in her application. In fact, several of her early readers commented on how much more confident she seemed in describing and analyzing her research than she had the previous year.

This is how the Enneagram helps us slice through the layers of those inner motivations that can feel so muddy and turn a situation that feels like an either/or into an integrated life. The Enneagram allows you to see with clarity *who you really desire to be* in a situation, as well as why certain struggles are likely to get under your skin. It gives you the resources both to step into new challenges and skillfully support yourself when you are struggling.

Defining the Enneagram

Enneagram means "nine-pointed figure" in Greek (a name that hints at its ancient origins). I have had thousands of conversations about the Enneagram since I first learned about this tool a decade ago. Some of these conversations have been with people who actually wanted to talk about it. Many were with anyone who happened to cross my path during that phase of my life when I first discovered the Enneagram and, with the zeal of a new convert, could not shut up about it.

I talked about it to my kid's friends' parents at the soccer game, my entire family and every colleague I've ever had. The Enneagram just always came up – about three questions in, if not sooner. The awkward name is always a struggle (it is pronounced "any-a-gram").

Have you ever fallen in love with a practice like this? Discovered a favorite yoga school – or a brain mapping book or a spiritual teacher – and held on tight because it gave you what you most needed? That is how I feel about the Enneagram. It is a teacher I trust and return to, again and again. Although it has roots in the Desert Mothers and Fathers of the Christian tradition and the Sufi or mystical branch of Islam, the Enneagram, as it is currently practiced, is not a religious tool but instead complements whatever spiritual or awareness path you are on.

My Enneagram Story

Despite all these conversations, what I have never shared before writing this book is more of my own personal story *vis-à-vis* the Enneagram. What have I experienced that is so powerful and what do I hope for you?

I first learned about the Enneagram when a friend paid for me to attend a workshop with Dallas-based Enneagram Master Suzanne Stabile. This was an all-weekend affair in which Suzanne described each of the nine types is detail, one by one, as we slowly worked our way around the circle, or Enneagram diagram (see page 50).

THE ENNEAGRAM

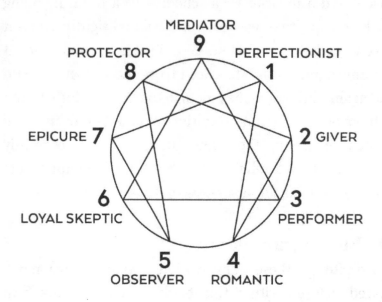

I had a hunch that I was a heart type. When she got to Type Three, which is also called the Performer, she started her description with these words: "Threes are the chameleons of the Enneagram." Kaboom! I knew I had been found.

She went on to describe more Type Three attributes. Threes are often leaders and organizers, we prioritize and focus on our work and have a hard time slowing down to enjoy life. We are extremely goal-oriented but don't hang around once the confetti drops on one of our goals, instead pressing ourselves forward onto the next one. The chameleon description points to the Three's habit of shape-shifting or turning into the poster child of any group to which we belong, however temporarily. We are very good at sensing the mood of the collective and becoming what you want us to be.

If this sounds familiar, Three may be your type. Many of my high-achieving clients also lead with Type Three. But it may not be. Hold that idea lightly while we continue to explore the Enneagram together. The U.S. is actually thought by many Enneagram teachers to be a Type Three country due to our emphasis on success and looking good. Dallas, my hometown, is also understood to be a Three town: all sparkle, little heart (or better put, a disconnection with one's own heart). If you are resonating with this Type Three description, it could just be a by-product or an overlay of the dominant culture.

Back at the weekend workshop, when Suzanne finished her description, she asked if anyone in the room thought they might be a Three. As I decided whether or not to raise my hand, I sat there excruciatingly aware of one painful detail. She had explained that Threes are often overdressed. (Looking good is very important for this personality type.) I looked down at my faux fur coat and the funky brooch that I had gotten as a gift for performing a wedding (it actually lit up and twinkled!) and thought, "This was probably a tiny bit too much for a Saturday afternoon at the learning center." I recognized that part of me that loved making an entrance.

Honestly, it was pretty uncomfortable to raise my hand (I was the only one) and claim that type. I felt really exposed. Not everyone feels this way, but Threes are in the shame/sadness triad (more on that in a minute), which likely helps explain my response. So please be kind to yourself if this process of identifying your type makes you feel vulnerable. On the other hand, you may feel super excited or curious or just neutral about discovering your type.

This is what the Enneagram has really helped to deliver me from: not just the ways I can shape-shift or morph to be what others want me to be, but also the way *I can be a chameleon to myself.* Not even letting myself know what I truly want. Going for the big credential over the tender nudge and doing what people want me to do, rather than risking my own truth.

In fact, for most of my twenties, I lived my life on two tracks: the real life and the resume life. For example, my four years in AmeriCorps and Peace Corps let me both pursue credentials (looks good on the grad school applications!) while actually building a life that responded to my heart's desires: meaningful, relational work that left space in the schedule for nature and creative projects, a simple life and housing and lots of time for personal growth, reading, yoga and friendships. The problem was that I thought I would have to leave all of that behind once I went to graduate school and became a grownup with a real career. This faulty mindset contributed to my burnout just three years after graduation.

I credit the Enneagram with being one of the most vital threads that pulled me out of the exhaustion pit and taught me how to hold my work and my time in a more sustainable way. On a daily basis, it helps me integrate my ambitions into the scope and pace of a life that feels good to be in. This is my hope for you.

A Brief and Poetic History of the Enneagram

What is the Enneagram? It is a map of the human experience that couples ancient spiritual teachings with contemporary lessons drawn from the fields of psychology and somatic (or body) awareness. It has origins in the deserts of North Africa and Egypt in the 4th century. At that time, spiritual seekers retreated from the extractive and dominating culture of the Roman Empire to live in caves and observe the human condition. They discovered that as human beings, we have nine different habitual ways of losing touch with our essential self and nine gifts that we are here to share (our Ennea types and our Ennea virtues.)

Without awareness, our personality is in the driver's seat of our lives. When we bring awareness to these personality habits (which live not only in our heads, but are full body neural pathways) we reconnect to the freedom and choice that is ours in each moment. And to the deeply intuitive voice of our essential self. This is a lifelong process but the Enneagram is a uniquely powerful tool to fast-track inner growth and awareness.

We are each born infused with our essential self. You can see this innate life force shine through when you hold a newborn or in tender interactions with people who are sick, dying or have a mental challenge that keeps them from hiding behind a socially constructed self.

But most of us can't bear to go through life that open and vulnerable because life can be rough. We get bumped and bruised and hurt, so we wrap ourselves in a package called personality. The problem is that we start to over-identify with the package. We come to think that we *are* the package and forget that there are more expansive versions of ourselves within — our deepest selves. From an Enneagram perspective, we call this our essence.

As children, with our nervous systems still developing, it truly does serve us to create a personality package. It would simply overload our circuits to remain completely open to life with all its intensity and rough edges. (Perhaps if we could learn to meditate at three or four we could swing it. My dream for the world!)

Filtering through our Enneagram perspective is *adaptive,* especially at the beginning. You could imagine the Enneagram personality as a cast that aids us in healing a primary wound. But at a certain point as adults, we have a choice. We are older, we have more wisdom and resources and fully-developed nervous systems. Now, it is not the wound that is affecting us, for the wound has long since healed. It is the cast, or the personality package, that limits our freedom of movement.

Again, the Enneagram identifies nine personality types: three types lead with their heart, three types lead with their head and three types lead with their gut or body knowing. We all tend to lead with one of these centers of intelligence, make significant use of another and underutilize the third.

You probably know and recognize certain people, friends or family members who might fall into these different categories: for example, the husband of your friend who is super analytical and seems to live in his head, or the aunt who is always helping and giving and loving even if you don't need what she offers. Or that quick-to-anger colleague who has an uncanny gut instinct. You may even have a natural sense about where you land, given these three categories.

The Two C's: Compassion and Curiosity

Before we help you figure out your type, I want to offer a few tips for getting the most out of this process. First of all, remember what I call the two C's: Compassion and Curiosity. You will know that you are holding this Enneagram tool in the right way if it 1) helps you feel more compassion for other people (and the way they are trapped in their own habits) and 2) it helps you have more compassion for yourself.

Compassion is vital because there is a serious danger that, as you learn the types, you will start labeling other people. It just comes up naturally: "Gah! That is totally my mom!" or "That is my husband," or "That's the coworker who drives me nuts."

It is fine to have a working hypothesis on what types you think some of the significant people in your life may be, as long as you remember that *no one can identify a type from the outside in.* Not even the most experienced Enneagram Master could tell you your type because it is rooted in motivation, not behavior. No one knows the motivation that drives the actions except for that person themselves. To me, this is very respectful.

As you recognize others in the Ennea type descriptions, please use those insights to relate to friends, family, and coworkers with more compassion, remembering that there are eight other perspectives on the world and eight other ways we trip ourselves up, again and again.

Remember that the most important and powerful Enneagram work you will do is with *yourself*. This is where you have the power to change things. Cultivating compassion for yourself may be the hardest part of all. The Enneagram journey is not a race to win or a hill to climb towards being a super healthy person (though it does help with that). It is a process of learning to relax your habitual responses to life in order to find more presence and freedom, moment-by-moment.

Also remember to hold the results from any online Ennea quiz lightly (especially the free ones). While they can be a starting point, the easiest way I have discovered to help people determine their type is to have them answer the three questions below and read a complete description of all nine types to see what resonates.

Really, the very best way to discover your type is to go to a weekend-long workshop and listen to panels of people from each type sharing their stories; but I'm assuming you may not have time to do that right now. If you do, I wholeheartedly recommend it and you can find one at www.enneagramworldwide.com. This site also has the best online quiz (for a nominal fee) – the only one that is scientifically developed and based on extensive research.

The second "C" is curiosity. You can't already know the answer and simultaneously be curious. Curiosity invites you into your beginner's mind. Observe what is happening in your life and the choices you make and their outcomes from this vantage point: "Hey, when I try that, this is what happens."

For example, when I don't push myself to keep writing but instead go take the nap that I want to take, I actually come back feeling much lighter and complete the chapter rather easily. (This just happened.) Remember the Enneagram doesn't put you in a box, it shows you the box that you are already in.

Lastly, watch out for feelings of overwhelm. The Enneagram is a very sophisticated, elegant and complex tool (which is why it is something you can come back to again and again throughout your life). However, as you read, remember that we aren't looking for this information to land in your head so much as listening for clues that will help you open up to yourself in a new way, gain perspective, feel more connected to others and put your suffering and struggles in a much larger perspective.

How to Determine Your Personality Type

Now, I will guide you through three questions that should help you identify your type or at least gift you a working hypothesis. I encourage you to grab a journal or piece of paper to write out the answers below. You will also find an Enneagram worksheet in my Flourish Kit at www.courtneypinkerton.com/flourishkit.

As a reminder, there are nine types divided into groups of three, or triads, based on whether the type leads with head, heart or gut intelligence.

ENNEAGRAM TRIADS

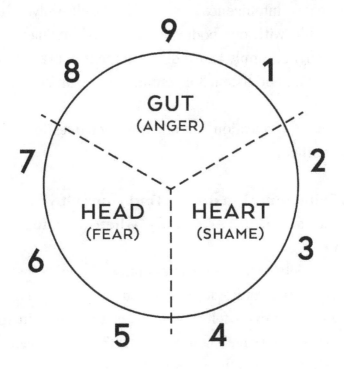

1. Do you filter life primarily through your head, heart, or gut/body?

How would a friend or a trusted family member describe you? (This is only a clue. Your type is based on motivation, not behaviors, so as we discussed above, you are the only one who can determine it.) Describe your "filter" or way of approaching the world.

In my experience, it can be easier for people to identify if they are a head or a heart person because we value those forms of intelligence more (the head most of all and emotional intelligence second). Culturally, our relationship with our bodies as a seat of intelligence is more fraught. Simply take a quiet moment to ask yourself this question and listen. Jot your answer down before you continue.

The second question is really the same question asked from another angle.

2. What emotion do you find yourself wrestling with most often, especially when you feel off-kilter?

Is it anxiety or fear – recurrent buzzy thoughts that feel like an internal radio station set on static? Is it shame, sadness or sorrow – felt physically as a pressure in your heart or an empty feeling in your chest? Or is it anger – a heat rising in the belly or resentment simmering in your gut? Describe this emotion, including how you feel it in your body.

We all feel all the emotions but one is more frequently under the surface for us. For head types (fives, sixes and sevens) it is fear, for the heart types (twos, threes, and fours) it is shame – sometimes also called sadness or grief – and for the gut or body types (eights, nines, and ones) it is anger.

3. In new social situations (imagine walking into a party where you know few people), how do you tend to react?

Would you turn it on, walk in and begin connecting to others, perhaps finding the host to introduce yourself? Or are you more likely to enter as unobtrusively as possible, to make your way around the edge of the gathering and look for a vantage point in the back to observe or connect to one person at a time? Or lastly, would you scan the environment, looking for the unspoken rules of this social scene and trying to identify something you can do to be useful, perhaps passing out nametags or helping the host?

This question is really about the energy that you would bring to the situation. Would you come blowing in strong (assertive), slink around the edges of the room (withdrawing) or try to play your appropriate part in that gathering (dutiful)? Describe your response in your journal or on your paper.

And now, with your answers to those three questions, you can discern your type or at least make an educated first guess. If you think you are a:

Head type and assertive, read more about Type Seven, the Epicure

Head type and withdrawing, check out Type Five, the Observer

Head type and dutiful, consider Type Six, the Loyal Skeptic

Heart type and assertive, read more about Type Three, the Performer

Heart type and withdrawing, check out Type Four, the Romantic

• **Heart type and dutiful**, consider Type Two, the Giver

Gut type and assertive, read more about Type Eight, the Protector

Gut type and withdrawing, check out Type Nine, the Mediator

Gut type and dutiful, consider Type One, the Perfectionist

A Tour of the Nine Types

Type One, the Perfectionists, believe that they must be good and right to be worthy. Consequently, Perfectionists are conscientious, responsible, improvement-oriented and self-controlled; they can also be critical, resentful and self-judging. They focus attention on what is right or wrong, correct or incorrect. The life lesson for this type is what is commonly called the "Serenity Prayer," to change what can be changed, to accept what cannot be changed and to develop the wisdom to know the difference. Ones are precise, clear, direct, honest and detail-oriented. Others may perceive Ones as judgmental, critical, sermonizing or closed-minded.

What do Type Ones tell us about themselves?

"I live with a powerful inner critic who constantly monitors my thoughts, words and deeds. I strive for perfection and feel responsible for making things right. I focus on being good while repressing my impulses and desires for pleasure. I get angry when important rules and standards are ignored or violated. I seek love and approval from others by being good and right."

• **Type Two, the Givers,** believe that you must give fully to others to be loved. Consequently, Givers are caring, helpful, supportive and relationship-oriented; they also can be prideful, intrusive and demanding. They focus their attention on others' needs, feelings and desires. The life lesson for this type is to develop the humility that comes from allowing yourself to be loved without being needed and to have some needs of your own. Twos are friendly, open, expressive, focused on others, and quick to support or give advice. Others may perceive Twos as overly helpful, nagging, controlling or resentful.

What do Type Twos tell us about themselves?

"I am preoccupied with the needs of others. I take pride in giving and helping. I sometimes feel that people take advantage of me. I have a hard time expressing my own needs. I can be manipulative and alter the ways in which I present myself to others."

Type Three, the Performers, believe that you must accomplish and succeed in order to be loved. Consequently, Performers are industrious, fast-paced, efficient and goal-oriented; they also can be inattentive to feelings, impatient and image-driven. This type focuses their attention on tasks, goals and recognition for accomplishments. The life lesson for Type Three is to reclaim the truth that love comes to you because of who you are and not because of what you do. Threes are enthusiastic, direct, topic-focused, fast-paced and confident. Others may perceive Threes as impatient, overly efficient, restrictive and overriding of others' views.

What do Type Threes tell us about themselves?
"I identify with accomplishment and success. My image drives my need to work hard and look good. I seek approval and acceptance on the basis of performance. I am highly competitive and love winning. I feel a constant pressure to perform."

Type Four, the Romantics, believe that you can regain the lost ideal love or perfect state by finding a love or situation that is unique, special and fulfilling. Consequently, Romantics are idealistic, deeply feeling, empathetic and authentic; they also can be dramatic, moody and self-absorbed. This type tends to focus their attention on what is missing. The life lesson for Type Fours is to reclaim the wholeness of the present moment by appreciating what is here and now, feeling the experience in their bodies rather than over-indulging in the story of what's happening and accepting themselves as they are, without needing to be special or unique. Fours are expressive of feelings, personal, self-focused and have a flair for originality. Others may perceive Fours as overly expressive, unsatisfied with responses and emotionally intense.

What do Type Fours tell us about themselves?
"I long for what's missing, distant or unattainable – the ordinary pales in comparison. My deep sense of

abandonment translates into a belief that I will never be fulfilled. I envy and idealize what others have that I don't. Authenticity and meaningful experiences are essential to me. My suffering sets me apart from others."

Type Five, the Observers, believe that they must protect themselves from a world that demands too much and gives too little. Consequently, Observers seek self-sufficiency and are non-demanding, analytic, thoughtful and unobtrusive; they also can be withholding, detached and overly private. They focus their attention on intellectual understanding, accumulating knowledge, and avoiding potential intrusions from others' agendas, needs and feelings. The life lesson for Type Fives is to reconnect to the vitality of your life force and your heartfelt feelings, realizing that ample energy and resources are available. Fives are content-focused, clear, analytical and wordy. They aren't big on "small talk." Others may perceive Fives as emotionally disconnected, aloof, over-analytical and distant.

What do Type Fives tell us about themselves?

"I have a strong need for privacy. I limit intrusion from a world that wants too much from me. I hoard time, space, energy, knowledge and myself. I detach from feelings and observe rather than participate. I am a minimalist."

Type Six, the Loyal Skeptics, believe that you must gain certainty and security in a hazardous world that you just can't trust. Consequently, Loyal Skeptics are intuitive, inquisitive, trustworthy, good friends and problem-solvers; they can also be doubtful, accusatory and fearful. They tend to focus their attention on what could go wrong, i.e. worst-case scenarios and how to deal with them. The life lesson for this type is to reclaim trust in yourself, in others and the world and live comfortably with uncertainty. Sixes are thoughtful, questioning, engaging and information-oriented. Others may perceive Sixes as pessimistic, contrary, challenging, doubting or controlling.

What do Type Sixes tell us about themselves?

"I am preoccupied with safety and security concerns. I greet everything with a doubting mind and contrary thinking. My vigilance, active imagination and intuition help me anticipate and avoid any and all problems. I question authority and people until they gain my trust. I procrastinate because I fear making the wrong decision."

Type Seven, the Epicures, believe that you must stay upbeat and keep your possibilities open to assure a good life. Consequently, Epicures seek pleasurable options and are optimistic and adventurous; they also avoid pain, and can be uncommitted and self-serving. This type focuses their attention on cultivating multiple options and idealized future plans. Their life lesson is to reclaim and accept all of life – the pleasures and the pains – in the present moment. Sevens are exuberant, fast-paced, spontaneous, analytical and idea-oriented. Others may perceive Sevens as quickly shifting topics, making excuses, self-absorbed and indifferent to the input of others.

What do Type Sevens tell us about themselves?

"Life is an adventure! I seek pleasure and have an insatiable appetite for new experiences. I am optimistic, active and energetic. I see multiple options but have difficulty with commitment. I do not like limits and avoid boredom."

Type Eight, the Protectors, believe that you must be strong and powerful to assure protection and regard in a tough world. Consequently, Protectors seek justice and are direct, strong and action-oriented; they also can be overly impactful, excessive and impulsive. They tend to focus their attention on injustice, not being controlled by others and getting things moving in work or play. The life lesson for this type is to harness their life force in productive ways, integrating self-assertion with vulnerability. Eights are direct, authoritative, zestful, firm, and oriented to truth and justice. Others may perceive Eights as confrontational, intimidating, loud and controlling.

What do Type Eights tell us about themselves?

"I thrive on having lots of energy in my body and enthusiasm for life. I am strong and I protect the weak. I am direct, willing to confront when the need arises, and express my anger immediately. People see me as aggressive, intimidating, intense and impulsive. I have trouble staying with my own vulnerability and sad feelings. I have a strong sense of knowing what is fair or right in my body center."

Type Nine, the Mediators, believe that to be loved and valued, you must blend in and go with the flow. Consequently, Mediators seek harmony and are inclusive, amiable, easy going, comfortable and steady; they also can be self-forgetting, conflict-avoidant and stubborn. This type focuses attention on other people's agendas and the external environment. Their life lesson is to reclaim yourself and wake up to personal priorities. Nines are non-confrontational, friendly, other-focused and inclusive of both feelings and facts. Others may perceive Nines as indecisive, scattered, unclear and overly conciliatory.

What do Type Nines tell us about themselves?

"As a harmonizer, I can see all sides to every issue. I avoid conflict and want a comfortable solution. I have difficulty saying "no" and can get resentful later for agreeing to something that I don't want to do. I am ambivalent or unsure about my own needs and wants. It's much easier to go along with others than to rock the boat." (Descriptions of the Enneagram types are adapted with permission from www.enneagramworldwide.com, Copyright 2018, The Narrative Enneagram.)

Remember, all the Ennea types struggle and all have potent gifts to share. In their purest forms, the Enneagram types are described only by numbers, which give our egos less on which to attach. Once we add descriptors, suddenly "Protector" sounds better than "Observer" and we can start trying to pick our type rather than letting it reveal itself to us.

The Enneagram and Stress

The Enneagram can help you identify motivations that keep you busy. For example, what might keep a Type Eight busy is that they want to control everything and it's hard to let others into their process. What might keep a Three busy is that they are extremely goal-oriented and want others to think well of them. Sevens don't want to miss out on any of life's experiences. Sixes want to live up to their internal standard for what a good person "should" do. Ones want to get it right. Twos want to be needed by others and so on.

It is also important to know that in times of stress and in times when you are feeling most secure or expansive, you may access or embody the energy of another type. This movement is illustrated by the inner lines on the Enneagram diagram (see page 50), which connect the type that you lead with to two other types. These complementary types are called the stress and security points or the disintegration and the integration points.

STRESS AND SECURITY TYPES

Leading	Stress	Security
1	4	7
2	8	4
3	9	6
4	2	1
5	7	8
6	3	9
7	1	5
8	5	2
9	6	3

In other words, if you are significantly stressed right now, you might look and feel like another type. The energy of our stress type often acts like a cold bucket of water on the dominant habit of our leading type. It wakes us up. For instance, when I was feeling stressed before resigning my job, I was having a hard time making decisions. Every option looked exactly the same. This is the energy of Type Nine, which worked to slow down my Type Three overachiever impulses to press on through to the next goal.

Although disorienting to me at the time, it was ultimately a valuable clue. Our "stress point" or "security point" energy need not only emerge during a dramatic or challenging time. I feel that same Nine energy – "I'm not sure what I want or need!" – when I am overwhelmed while shopping with three kids at Costco.

Helpful Tips on Typing

To discern your type, listen for the basic pattern which has been true for most of your life. It is also important to know that, in general, we acquire personality habits for the first half of life and for the second half of life we tend to be shedding them. If you are having a hard time typing yourself, it can be helpful to think of yourself in college or in your young adulthood (if you're past that time in your life); that is often when your personality is at its strongest.

If you had met me when I was twenty-one, I might have looked much more like the Three archetype than I do now. I lived in London that year, studying at the London School of Economics, completely camouflaging myself (remember the chameleon?) in black and absorbing British inflections in an effort to blend in. I relished travelling because every train station and airport felt like a little stage for my one-woman show. I loved crafting outfits that made me feel glamorous and cosmopolitan and like I had it all pulled together.

For me, it was really the experience of childbirth that woke me out of some of the Three performance habits that I had been engaged in for most of my twenties. I was very disconnected from my body and very much in my head when I had our son Coleman, halfway through four years of grad school. The whole experience did not go the way I expected in large part because birth is not something that you can force your way through or perform. It is much more a process of surrendering to your body and its wisdom – something I had very little practice doing. (More on this in Chapter 7: Understand the Language of Your Body.)

In your own journey, you may find that you have been learning to wake up and shed some of your Enneagram habits naturally. That just confirms that you are on the right path. Life has a way of raising those lessons for us and inviting us to wholeness. Now with the Enneagram, you have a roadmap for doing it even more consciously.

Your Gift to Share

After all that Enneagram exploring, let's land with something beautiful and concrete, shall we? Hopefully, now you have at least a working hypothesis for your type. When I teach the Enneagram at events or to a new coaching client, I like to end the session with sharing the qualities of essence, or virtues – the unique contribution that each type offers to the world. Many of my clients find it reassuring to know that the very same aspects of their personality that have tripped them up most in their lives – their personality bias – can be converted into a gift that they can share with others.

The truth is that **your gift and your bias are the same inner attribute**, the thing that your soul loves and holds dearest. It is just that when we are all tight and grasping inside, we hold this energy in a constricted way, which creates our personality bias. We don't do this on purpose, of course; it's just a habit born out of a fear that we won't in fact have what we need or long for. But when we learn to relax back into our fullest experience, we remember that reality is much bigger than we see it through our particular Ennea specs. And from this place of openness we embody our gift, without even trying. Seriously, it often feels like a surprise: "I've spent how long chasing this thing only to discover it is right here, closer even than my own breath?"

The Qualities of Essence

Type One (Perfectionist) – Serenity. An internal balance and grounded heart to respond to life's changes gracefully.

Type Two (Giver) – Humility. That simple recognition that, like us all, you too have needs and limitations.

Type Three (Performer) – Authenticity. The capacity to create a life that is more and more congruent with your heart.

Type Four (Romantic) – Equanimity or spaciousness of heart. Room inside for all the emotions to flow without getting stuck in any of it.

Type Five (Observer) – Non-attachment. Being really present to everything because it is temporary and precious.

Type Six (Loyal Skeptic) – Courage. The capacity to live one's own truth day in and day out. The courage of everyday life.

Type Seven (Epicure) – Sobriety / Constancy. Simply enjoying and being fed by the moment with a satisfied and fulfilled heart.

Type Eight (Protector) – Innocence. A big, beautiful and open heart.

Type Nine (Mediator) – Engagement or right action. The capacity to show up and make your mark.

PRACTICE: Fieldwork for Each Type

Below are some recommended awareness practices or fieldwork, one for each type. (You will find more practices in Chapter 9: Immerse Yourself When Stress Builds.)

Type One: The Inner Critic is Not Your Friend. We all have an inner critical voice but for Type One, that voice is really developed. See if you can become more familiar with the critic while distancing yourself from its messages. Where does it hang out and what does it tend to say? This voice is only interested in its own survival and in keeping things the same, not in your wellbeing. (For more on the inner critic see Chapter Seventeen in *Deep Living: Transforming Your Relationship to Everything that Matters Through the Enneagram* by Roxanne Howe-Murphy.)

Type Two: Bring it Back Home. Notice the way your attention so easily goes to other people and their needs. See if you can invite it back home and gift yourself some time and space for self-care. Some Enneagram types need to get up and get moving. You need some time on the couch. Make a concrete plan every week for some self-care: massage, reading in the bath or a walk by yourself. Practice taking care of yourself the same way you so generously care for others.

Type Three: Shift Your Center of Gravity from Outside to Inside. Set a reminder on your phone to go off two or three times a day. Once it does, stop what you are doing and put your hand over your heart (even if this sounds way too cheesy, hang with me). Simply let yourself breathe and be curious about what is going on inside for you. Be patient with this practice. At first, it can feel like nothing is there but as you relax that habit of freezing your heart to get the work done you can tune in even better to those subtle sensations and continue to pay attention to what touches and nourishes you.

Type Four: Act on Your Gifts. Fours can struggle with being judgmental and perfectionists, which makes it hard for them to actually claim their real talents. If it feels overwhelming to take meaningful action to use your gifts in the world, create small steps and move forward on them, one day at a time. Remember you don't have to feel a certain way to take action. Simply take the action anyway because the world needs your gifts.

Type Five: Awaken Your Body with Movement. Commit to a regular physical practice: yoga, Aikido and other martial arts, bicycling, hiking and dancing are all good options. Choose whatever you enjoy. Find a regular way (consistency is key) to quicken your body and let all that energy in your head flow back into your limbs and awaken them. This can change everything. We engage with life in and through our bodies, not just through our eyes and heads.

Type Six: Key into the Positive. Each day, notice what is working well in your life. This could be a gratitude list or a reflection in the shower on the many types of gifts that you enjoy. I know gratitude lists can feel forced but this is simply a practice to take the attention away from planning for the worst possible scenarios (a habit of this type), direct it to what is already going well and key into how it feels to trust yourself to handle whatever comes up.

Type Seven: Find Your Ommmm. Whether it is a walking practice, a coloring-in-mandalas practice or a traditional sitting meditation, find a regular meditation practice that works for you. This will allow your busy mind to relax some of its anticipation and mental chatter and help you build your capacity to observe and be with the full range of body sensations and emotional experiences as they emerge. (Chapter 9 on immersion offers a simple "pebbles in your pocket" practice, which is a great meditation for Type Sevens.)

Type Eight: Play with your Energy. Eights tend to bring a big amount of energy to every task. Instead, see if you can modulate. Feel into the difference between the energies required to pick up a kitten versus beat back an adversary. See if you can modulate the energy that you bring to match the specific task at hand.

Type Nine: What's In It For You? At the beginning of each day, feel into your own priorities. Name at least one (the MIT exercise in Chapter 5 is helpful here). Write it on a sticky note and *do it*. (This builds trust with yourself that you can follow through.) Notice if you tend to back away from your chosen priority when you receive any resistance. Remember that your life works best when you are willing to show up and make your marks.

My client Dylan leads with Type Nine on the Enneagram, so her virtue is engagement or right action. In addition to working out, going to sleep earlier, giving herself to work more and gaining recognition in the process, it is beautiful to see how she is thriving in her life the more she shows up and initiates things. She has recently decided to try to get pregnant with her second baby and was just featured on NPR because of a powerful cultural essay that she wrote. Literally, the more she remembers that her voice really matters (our world isn't complete without it), the more her life blooms. This is the way out of the box that we forgot we were in.

5 LEARN TO HAVE A LOVE AFFAIR WITH YOUR WORK

If we really want to reinvent our schedules to make space for what is most important to us, we have to understand what filled them up in the first place. One of the most common pain points I see with clients is how they relate to their work. In Step L of the Flourish process, we explore and shift our relationship to work in order to create breathing room both in our routine and from the internal pressures that push us constantly.

As you read this chapter, know that you don't have to make any dramatic changes in your work or your routine yet. We will talk about how to know when it's the right time for a big move later. Remember, slowing down is simply a phase in the transformational process that allows you to find freedom from old habits that no longer serve you and create new ones. The point is to shift from feeling like you have to push and strive and strain against life to instead feeling so buoyed up by the life you have created that your most important gifts naturally emerge.

Also remember that this chapter and all the steps in the Flourish process include multiple tools to aid you in your self-exploration. Some, like the Enneagram, are more conceptual. They help you internalize fresh frameworks and understand your lived experiences in new ways. This helps you approach your choices differently. Others, like the MITs or Most Important Tasks, described in this chapter, are more concrete. While simple, these practices create interior space for you to hear your deeper wisdom and take action.

Both conceptual and concrete tools help you move with more ease (and more quickly) out of the places of constriction and suffering and into a life that is more and more congruent with your deepest purpose: the work that is yours and yours alone to do. When you are ready, either as you move through the chapter or later when you complete the book, I do invite you to spend some time with the exercises you find here. They are game changers.

Self-Awareness: The Compassionate Inner Observer

Throughout this book, I suggest observing yourself. What exactly am I talking about? We all have inner voices. I used to think this made me crazy. Now I know that it makes me (and you) one hundred percent human. The inner critic, the inner saboteur, the inner overachiever who thinks she has to earn the gold star to get the love – they are all in there. These voices stem from the ego or the protective layer of personality wrapped around our deepest, most essential self. Yet you can observe these voices without believing them; in fact, this is where the magic lies. This practice is called "cultivating your compassionate inner observer."

Inner voices can be harshly critical and judgmental. Sometimes they masquerade as your friend – pushing you forward when you would rather hang back or challenging you to "get it right." That is why it is so important to remember to connect to your *compassionate* inner voice. Compassion is a hallmark of the true inner observer. It doesn't need you to already be better. It is neutral. Your inner observer is simply a vantage point from which you can watch the other voices play out without choosing to follow them. It offers respite. And like a muscle, the more we practice this particular awareness technique and choose to align our perspective with our inner observer, the stronger it becomes.

Why is this so important? Because once we can observe ourselves without following the directives of all those faux inner voices, we can break out of the autopilot that defines so many women's lives – what I call the "busyness fog" – and approach our lives with more presence. For example, I recently concluded a long-term volunteer role. It was a mutually celebrated ending and time for fresh leadership to take my place; but I have felt the absence of that meaningful role in my life and struggled with feeling like I "should" be volunteering.

Last night I went outside in the backyard after dark (I have my best conversations with myself when no one is looking). Gazing up into the night sky made it easier to connect to my inner observer. From this more spacious perspective, I could really feel my need for rest. I could see the fullness of my work commitments right now and my desire to focus on completing this book and planning an upcoming retreat.

The inner observer reminds me that I don't need to heed that voice that says I *should* be doing more. The inner observer is always about acknowledging what is here right now: our current habits, patterns, thoughts and emotions. It helps us remember that we get to choose which inner prompts we follow and what we let into our lives and our schedules.

What's In It For You?

The best spiritual or truth teachers I have encountered always direct me back to my own lived experience. They say, "Don't take my word for it. Discern the truth of this teaching for yourself." This is my advice to you: Experiment with the inner observer. Take note of your own inner voices, especially as they pertain to work and more broadly *what you should be doing*. Get curious about what might be motivating you to fill your schedule. Don't judge yourself, just zoom out to observe the whole pattern.

Another way to approach this self-observation is to ask, *"What's in it for you to keep filling your life with commitments (even fun or social ones)?"* What payoff does living this way offer, even if it is one that you don't readily acknowledge to yourself? Does it make you feel important? Does it impress your friends and family? Does it keep you from looking at the parts of your life that might not be going as well? Whatever it is, if we can identify the subterranean impulses that press you forward, we can help you unhook from this habit of speeding through your days or otherwise engaging life on autopilot and all the discomfort that it generates.

The Pain of Work Envy

I have a hunch that one reason you stay busy has something to do with work envy or the impulse to keep up with other people's accomplishments. This habit keeps us caught in a perpetual web of comparing and despairing, as we argue with the internal judge or evaluator who finds us lacking and say, "Look at everything I got done today! Take that!"

However isolated and unhappy we may feel when in the grip of this comparing mind, work envy represents a universal human desire to use our gifts well and to position ourselves favorably against others. As Alain de Botton explains in his book *Status Anxiety*: "The hunger for status, like all appetites, can have its uses: spurring us to do justice to our talents, encouraging excellence, restraining us from harmful eccentricities and cementing members of a society around a common value system. But, like all appetites, its excesses can also kill."

De Botton goes on to explain that unlike romantic love, which gets so very much play in popular culture, our longing for "love from the world" via a meaningful and inspired relationship with our work, is largely ignored:

Every adult life could be said to be defined by two great love stories. The first – the story of our quest for sexual love – is well known and well charted, its vagaries form the staple of music and literature, it is socially accepted and celebrated. The second – the story of our quest for love from the world – is a more secret and shameful tale. If mentioned, it tends to be in caustic, mocking terms, as something of interest chiefly to envious or deficient souls, or else the drive for status is interpreted in an economic sense alone. And yet this second love story is not less intense than the first, it is no less complicated, important or universal, and its setbacks are no less painful. There is heartbreak here too.

In other words, we are encouraged to focus or pursue romantic love. This is seen as a normal human desire or impulse. But our relationship with work is often portrayed only in terms of financial compensation or material gain.

Absolutely, receiving money or earning a livelihood is an important part of any thriving relationship with work. But there are more ingredients to a true love-affair: things like self-expression, creativity, personal satisfaction and getting to feel that we are (and are seen as) people who show up authentically *even in our professional roles*. A love affair with work is rooted in fidelity to your best self and in the feeling that you are being faithful to your gifts. And like any passionate love affair, it does sometimes go down in flames.

So how can we metabolize this heartbreak and instead discover a meaningful, loving relationship with our work? First, we need to help you find freedom from work envy by decoding its helpful message for you.

The Compare and Despair Economy

Work envy is a tender topic and one with which I am quite familiar. While I don't find myself a particularly jealous person in other realms of life, when it comes to observing the professional success of others I have a slightly evil inner persona who emerges and hijacks my attention. And even worse, I'm ashamed of her.

For example, in the last few years I've found myself envious of female authors being interviewed about their books on NPR. I think that type of envy is pretty obvious; in a backward way, it points to my desire to write a book that contributes to the public discourse about issues I care about. But work envy can also pop up in relation to much smaller things.

For example, several years ago, a new neighbor blew into and out of my life within a few months. We had both just had babies. We started women-oriented businesses at the same time. We developed an insta-friendship born out of these commonalities and our proximity down the road from each other. Maybe it was because of the hormones but I reverted to a high-schooler in her presence, feeling awash in insecurities and competition.

After a particularly charged conversation, we had a friendship breakup. I'm not sure either of us understood what exactly happened other than we had somehow gotten all twisted up and needed more space. That was a tumultuous time in my life (immediately before and after my decision to leave my job) and I think the friendship mirrored my inner confusion.

Recently, someone asked for a referral that made me think of my former friend/neighbor (who had since moved away) so I googled her business to share the contact info. Scanning through her website, I was super proud of her and all that she has done. However, I felt a squeeze right around my heart space and a gurgle in my belly as I watched the gorgeous intro video on her website.

"I want a gorgeous, professionally edited video on my website," my inner envy monster said. "I only have silly YouTube videos, which don't look nearly as fabulous," she goes on to say.

In moments like these, we have a choice. We can try to outrun the envy monster or we can make space to really *feel* into her, which is what allows us to learn what we need to learn. (More on how to extract the helpful message from work envy in a bit.)

It is so important to retrain ourselves here because this habit of comparing is honestly one of our biggest distractions. It keeps us from truly thriving in our lives and generates huge amounts of suffering.

It can be hard for recovering overachievers to find and hold onto satisfaction in our work lives because, truthfully, we are never quite done. We never fully arrive. We are never impressed by our own accomplishments. Speaking for myself, I am currently writing a book which is due in a month, teaching a retreat to one hundred women in four days and marketing an international women's retreat (along with hopefully raising up three children, loving my man, and helping to organize our school garden).

Does my inner evaluator find this impressive? Nope. She wants a pretty video. Right now. Do you see the trap? Work envy fuels to-do lists that will never be done and that require us to sprint through our own lives.

Maybe your industry is not about pretty websites and instead there is another currency you use to compare and despair. But whether it is the news about a famous author or thought leader in your field or competition with a friend or colleague, with social media it can feel like we are surrounded by the news of others' successes 24/7.

If you let yourself scan back over the last few days or weeks, where has work envy shown up in your life? How do you tend to treat it when it appears? Work envy is the secret rocket fuel for so many overachievers. It propels us forward at an unsustainable pace because if you are running to catch up to someone else's life, it inevitably creates friction and suffering in your own.

What else can we choose to do with all that tangled up envy energy? First of all, drop the attention on the other person. As many times as you need to, drop it. This is not about them, it is about *you*. And in a funny way, this person is doing you a service. Often, she is waking you up to a desire that you didn't yet know you had. Something deep and interior or something you haven't been acknowledging fully to yourself.

Maybe you're like my client Abby who found herself irritated at the book contract garnered by her friend, which helped Abby recognize her desire to publish about her recent adventures traveling globally with her family. Or Hilary, who heard that the keynote speaker for the medical conference she was attending was a young woman like herself and wondered, "What makes her so qualified?" Upon further inquiry, Hillary realized that she, too, longed for more speaking opportunities.

What are the kinds of things that make you envious of others' work accomplishments? Is it the awards? The media coverage? Praise from a boss or a mentor? Lifestyle things, like the fact that they get to travel for their work or wear better clothes? Creative contributions like getting their podcast showcased on a high-profile website or their painting picked up by a respected gallery? What else? What hidden interest, goal or passion might the envy be highlighting for you? Is it showing you something you long for?

Simply acknowledging this latent desire is a huge step in the right direction even if you don't yet know what to do or how to invite it into your life. Why? Sometimes overachievers can be afraid to name their juiciest personal goals even if they are already super accomplished. It can be easier to stay in the zone of checking off things you know you are good at or that impress others rather than to stretch after a heart-felt desire you aren't sure you can achieve. This stems from a fear of failure.

Decoding work envy and bringing those true longings to the surface allows you to see and claim your most sacred goals – the things that matter most to *you*. And when we drop our focus on the other woman *and what she has* it frees up an enormous amount of energy, which you can now direct toward your true soul goals. Magic!

I also need to clarify that it is totally *fine* if you are harboring a desire that you haven't fully acknowledged. Most of us don't grow up educated or steeped in the ways of this inner compass. We don't live in a culture that teaches us how to map our desires and trust them. The last thing we need for you is to beat yourself up for not always knowing and acknowledging your dreams. Seriously, it doesn't help.

Beyond revealing latent goals or desires, work envy may also be pointing to a deeper lesson: your need to stop looking outside of yourself for validation. It is an invitation to relax the habit of finding your worthiness in the reflection of another gold star.

I had a moment of clarity about this when I was in the Peace Corps in Nicaragua, where I worked primarily with women to help start cooperative projects, like small businesses, neighborhood improvements and community banks.

As I was just getting my bearings, I met a Canadian who was part of a nonprofit organization promoting similar rural projects for women. I developed a total work envy/work crush on her. First of all, she was Canadian. (Am I the only one who has wanted to pretend she was Canadian while travelling just to avoid having to defend the international politics of the U.S.?) Secondly, she seemed to have a "real job." whereas my Peace Corps gig was only for a set two-year period. Plus, she was super cute and stylish in an effortless-seeming "I just threw this on to hike up the volcano, empower some women, and star in my own lifestyle biopic" kind of way.

The Canadian and I would bump into each other from time to time in the larger town where I went to buy groceries and we would compare notes. One day, she told me that she had made it out to one of the outlying communities to present a lesson on medicinal plant cooperatives. To this, my internal response was "Damn. I was planning to make it out to that community to teach about medicinal plant cooperatives. She got there first."

I literally felt like throwing up while writing that last sentence. But there it is. Forget the fact that we were working in the second poorest country in the western hemisphere. Forget that there were literally hundreds of tiny communities around full of brave, inventive and very, very marginalized people. I had to be in some sort of race or competition with this woman.

It was such a sad internal moment that it shocked me out of my autopilot and set me on a path to first *understand* and ultimately to find freedom from work envy. This same journey is possible for you. I hope this confession/case study from my life helps you be gentler with yourself around your own feelings of work envy as they occur. When we shame or guilt ourselves for making these comparisons, we end up driving those painful thoughts in deeper.

Instead of nurturing the envy, the next time it appears, try to make some space for it and hold your humanity with kindness. Then see if you can decode the envy as outlined above. Is it calling your attention to a dormant desire? Or showing you where you need to unhook from the praise of others? Either way, metabolizing work envy can be one of the quickest ways for you to begin to feel radically different (and better) in your everyday life.

PRACTICE: *Mudita* ("Sympathetic Joy") Meditation

Beyond asking the questions above, how else can we move beyond feeling that life is a zero-sum game, holding on to the painful idea that each accomplishment that another woman marks off her list somehow diminishes our worth? Increasingly, I think that celebrating another's pleasure and success may be one of the fastest ways we draw it into our own lives. To cultivate this new approach, try this simple meditation adapted from a Buddhist practice called *mudita* or "Sympathetic Joy." You can download a guided *mudita* meditation as part of the Flourish Kit, a free collection of resources available at www.courtneypinkerton.com/flourishkit.

First, find somewhere comfortable to be and sit in a relaxed yet alert way, with your spine elongated so that you can breathe easily. Allow yourself to just be in the silence for a few breaths, observing the state of your body, emotions and mind. How are you feeling today? Just make space for what emerges.

Then, once you are ready, call to mind a friend who has something to celebrate in their life: a new job, house, baby, book or other creative project, a new travel opportunity, etc. It can be anything; however, if you want to supercharge this practice, focus on a friend who received something *that you also desire*. For example, I have a friend who is my business accountability buddy. While we work in different fields she and I are both scaling our businesses this year and have new income goals related to this growth. I just got news that she signed a high-profile client. I spent a few quiet moments engaged in a *mudita* practice. Although the meditation focused on her, I believe this kind of celebration opens the door both for gratitude for what you currently have and invites more of what you want into your life. I'll be real with you: It is not always easy. In fact, sometimes this practice can feel a little forced; but stick with it. It gets easier and really breaks the habit of comparing and despairing and helps you release those feelings and thoughts when they do show up.

After you have selected the friend and the accomplishment, imagine that you can offer them these phrases as if they were really in front of you and you could celebrate with them. "May your good fortune/success continue. May your happiness increase. May your life shine."

Feel free to put these mantras in your own words. The point is to nurture *a genuine feeling of happiness inside of you, for them.* Continue to breathe deeply as you extend these phrases, simply noticing how you feel in your body.

Next, call to mind a neutral person, someone whose name you may not even know but with whom you interact regularly. I like to think of an elderly gentleman who sits in his rocker a few doors down each evening. Perhaps, for you it is the waiter at your favorite restaurant, the nurse at your pediatrician's office or a friend of a friend. Trust whoever bubbles up and again, imagine them in front of you as if you could offer them personally these wishes: "May your good fortune/success continue. May your happiness increase. May your life shine."

If you want to challenge yourself, you can continue and call to mind someone whose success makes you a little green. This could be someone you know (a colleague or friend) or a public figure you find yourself envying. Again, offer them the well wishes and simply observe what comes up for you as you do. If you find it hard to do, you can also imagine yourself next to them, only instead of offering yourself the mantra for increased success, you can simply drink in gratitude for all the things, big and small, you have to celebrate.

End the celebration with a global sentiment, "May the happiness and satisfaction of all increase further and further."

Often, we think of sympathy only in terms of feeling another's pain. This practice challenges that idea and lets us revel also in another's successes and pleasure. It breaks down the idea that we are all in this alone and instead invites us to enjoy our interconnection, dropping us out of the comparing mind and softening our heart. This enhances our capacity to savor the celebrations and accomplishments in our own lives, as well.

Your Hero's Journey

What fuels work envy is actually a passion that springs from a deep and beautiful place. You care about our world. You also know that you have been entrusted with gifts and talents that you want to express fully. Elizabeth Gilbert, the author of *Big Magic,* explains in her blog:

> The word "talent" comes to us from the ancient Greek word for a sum, a balance, or a weight. In the Roman Empire, a talent was a unit of currency. You were paid, in other words with a certain amount of talent — your salary, your allotment, your share.
>
> And so it is with our creative or intellectual or physical or emotional gifts, whatever they may be. We are ALL paid in some kind of talent or another when we arrive here on earth – a different sort of talent for all, and a different amount of talent for all. Some of us get a few coins; some of us get a sack of gold. But everyone gets something. ("How

are you spending your talent?" by Elizabeth Gilbert, published on Oct 29, 2013.)

In Greek classics like *The Iliad* and *The Odyssey*, we encounter characters giving it their all on the field of life. I remember reading these epic poems as an eighteen-year-old on the verge of college and thinking to myself, "Yes! I relate to this passion, the quest for adventure and the intensity of these stories. I am hungry for that in my own life!" I suspect that you recognize something familiar in the hero's quest and resonate with their vision and capacity to go beyond what most people are willing to do.

These are beautiful attributes that not everyone shares. Seriously, some people actually need to stoke their internal fires and allow themselves a little more ambition. They need encouragement that their work and contributions matter to our collective story. This is not your struggle. You know that you have something beautiful to contribute, you just want to know exactly what that is and how to offer it in a way that doesn't consume your whole life. Your internal heat is part of your original medicine, those unique healing gifts that you bring to the world. Interestingly, we are always our first patient. We mend ourselves and then naturally, out of a place of being filled up to overflowing, we share the balm with others. Without even trying, your authentic life can then be an encouragement to others.

Have a Love Affair with Your Work

How could it shift things for you to take the invitation of this chapter seriously and to begin to view your work as a relationship? A love affair that is compelling and consuming and that requires attention, care and a certain degree of trust and surrender? A relationship of give and take, of surprises and stretches. In the same way that partners can be mirrors of our deepest-held habits (and things we might otherwise be blind to), our relationship to work can be a powerful teacher.

But what if your work feels less like a teacher than a tormentor? If that's true for you right now, ask yourself this question: *"Is this the right work for me? Am I deeply drawn to it? Does it make me feel seen, cherished and challenged in the same way I would expect from a romantic partner?"* If the answer is no... you have choices but they all start with noticing it and making space for your current experience.

When I was truly struggling with my work, a wise mentor suggested that I find a symbol of the wholeness and growth I wanted in work and in my whole life. She told me that it can help to have a concrete physical reminder. I chose a tulsi, or holy basil seedling I had just planted in my herb garden. Each day as I watered it, I heard my mentor's voice, questions and reminders in my head. She told me: You are making the commitment to thrive. It is now simply a question of whether you can grow and bloom in your current work relationship or if you need to find another container. When or if it is time to go you will know. And she was right! So if you are currently really unhappy at work I encourage you to create a daily reminder and to engage in a similar process of inquiry. Trust your own sense of timing and this self-reflection will, step by step, lead you toward the work that most inspires you and shares your biggest, brightest gifts.

If you really like your work but are still struggling, the next question is: *"Am I requiring my work to give me more than it can give?"* For we can get all the externals lined up perfectly: dream job, dream life and dream colleagues. But if we continue to approach our work needing approval from the world all the time, we will inevitably get hurt.

Likewise, even good work can't comprise a full and satisfying life, all by itself. Say you enjoy your work; do you let it set all the terms? Do you check email first thing and before you go to bed? Rarely take vacation or full weekends off? If so, you are bound to build up some resentment in your relationship to work – which is your invitation to pay attention to the other areas of life: creativity, spirituality, relationships, body/wellness etc. and infuse your schedule with activities and respite that you enjoy.

Engaging in work as a love affair shifts your focus from other people, either as competitors or fans, and allows you to acknowledge how precious your work is to *you, which paves the way for you to find your own satisfaction in it.* I learned this lesson recently talking to my virtual assistant Eileen, who is also a skilled photographer. She helped with a Flourish retreat I hosted in Mexico and took some amazing photos of the event, including some of me.

As my life and work continued to evolve – including doing a wholesale overhaul of my website to correspond with the publishing of this book – I realized I needed a new photo shoot. I felt awkward about this as I was planning to bring in a portrait photographer and these new photos would essentially replace the photos Eileen took, so I talked with her about it.

Eileen's response was great. She told me it is totally natural to need fresh photos (and gave examples of authors and coaches she knows who have a photo shoot every six months). She also said "I am really proud of the photos I took and I know that you enjoyed them." Boom. I felt that in my chest when she said it. I realized that Eileen *knows the value of her own work* and thus is not overly attached to exactly how these pictures are used or the timeframe in which I use them. She knows for herself that she created beauty and made her mark. She can let the work be what it needs to be and live for the time it needs to live. A dose of nonattachment, coupled with a deep valuing of our own work, is how we untangle from the pain of proving and pushing and striving and instead get to *enjoy* our work.

It's also important to remember that you do not have complete control. Our best work always requires a dance partner of some sort – an inspiration that comes to us from beyond the realm of our small minds or an organization or colleague who helps us bring our work to life. There is also the question of timing. Sometimes our best ideas need to ripen until we and our communities or contexts are ready for them. In this way, our work is a dance with life and with factors beyond our control, to which we are constantly responding.

Offer Your Work in a "Palms Open" Way

How do we nurture this love affair with our work? One strategy is to practice offering your best efforts in what I call a "palms open way" – not needing to get approval or positive feedback in return. (This, by the way, is another aspect of the compare and despair economy. Not only do we look to others and evaluate ourselves as lacking, we also judge what we are doing constantly against some external measure of success.)

Of course, it's impossible to try to hold this "palms open" posture all the time. We do care. Pretending to be unattached to the outcome isn't honest. But even being aware of how much we care and stepping back a bit from that edge (like putting the phone in the drawer when all we want to do is refresh Facebook to see how many "likes" we got) will bring us perspective and relief. Because if we are only ever giving to get or competing in our work, it will always eat whatever boundary we try to set between it and our personal lives.

Below, I offer my three favorite strategies for shifting your relationship to work and finding the freedom to flourish in your *whole* life: Creating Your Life-Giving Morning Routine, MITs (Most Important Tasks) and NNTs (Non-Negotiable Time). These are examples of fieldwork practices that I customize for clients as part of my Flourish eight-step coaching program. I call them fieldwork because like the birder headed out to the forest or the scientist tracking migration patterns in the field, they are your invitation to get curious and observe what happens in the eco-climate of your everyday life when you introduce these processes. What shifts?

PRACTICE: Your Life-Giving Morning Routine

For most of us, the morning routine is the hinge point between home and work and, as such, it is a powerful tool that helps us shape our days. In Peace Corps, I would wake up and encounter the grandmother of my host family asking me the same question each day: *"¿Cómo amaneció?"* It took me several weeks to understand her but finally, I caught on. This was the Nicaraguan version of good morning! In a literal sense, it translates to "How did you dawn?" I love the poetry in this phrase. I have always been a morning person. Not an extreme morning person like my Granny who would get up with the light and put in a couple of hours gardening before I rolled out of bed on summer vacation (she was probably onto something). But I like the morning nonetheless.

One week recently, I got up extra early to drive to teach at a retreat center. And I surprised myself by pausing to make my bed in the predawn darkness. I couldn't not do it. To leave the bed unmade felt like a rumpled start to my day. As I observed this process, I realized, "Wow. I guess this is now part of my morning routine!"

It certainly hasn't always been. For years, I went for the shabby chic look (at least that was what I told myself it was) of simple, monotone covers tousled in a relaxed way. And who knows, when my kids are older, I may just want the freedom to flop down on the bed anytime I desire without pulling back the covers. But for now, as my de-cluttering and de-owning streak continues, I can't get enough of smooth surfaces.

Spiritual teachers agree that a morning routine is vital. In fact, how we start the day is intimately connected with how we will end it. Here are a couple of tips to make your routine more powerful:

Design your routine around practices that genuinely appeal to you. This seems obvious but sometimes people choose practices because someone else recommended them or they think they should. I run into this frequently with meditation students who say, "I *should* be meditating... or doing a gratitude journal," or whatever. Scrap all that. Just listen for one thing that genuinely feels yummy.

Some examples include: five minutes of listening to the birds with your first cup of coffee, a few minutes to journal in a favorite chair, squeezing a fresh lemon and enjoying warm lemon water to wake up your senses (and boost your immunity), an eight to twenty-minute meditation sit, a nature walk looking at the beauty around you, ten guilt-free minutes to cuddle with your beloved, a child or a pet.

The point is to simply choose a practice that reminds you that this is *your* life and gets you out of a mode of reacting to external pressures. (Bonus points if you can manage to leave your phone in a drawer and avoid checking email and social media until later in the day. A simple alarm clock, even though it feels like a throwback to an earlier era, is a great aid here.)

Give your routine room to breathe. Like all spiritual practices, our morning routine is organic and changes over time. The important thing is to be attentive, to notice when something wants to be incorporated and to let it in. Likewise, let go of practices when the time is right to make space for the new.

Last spring, I was wrestling with my morning meditation because it wanted to grow to include time for yoga before I sat. You know what my inner overachiever thinks about this use of time, right? She has work to get to! Finally, I realized it wasn't worth ignoring the inner nudge anymore. My body wants to move before it can easily meditate, write or hold space for a coaching client. So I let it – and I tell my inner overachiever to simmer on down. Some days, she even listens.

My Morning Routine

The big breakthrough for me was to think of my routine in two parts. There is what I do before I take my children to school and after I drop them off. You may have other factors that divide your mornings in a similar way. Maybe it's before you get to work and after you get to work, or before and after you exercise, so make this process your own. Below is a tour of my morning routine. I hope it helps you design one that is just right for you.

Before I take the kids to school. Enjoy lemon water and ten minutes to journal in bed. Make my bed. Make a pot of tea and enjoy a cup while I braid hair and otherwise wrangle children. The rest goes in my thermos for the road. (Because it's the details that make a tour fun, I'll tell you I am currently on a jag of Red Chai Masala tea in an effort to drink less caffeine. Perennial favorites are yerba mate, a smoky green tea and tulsi, which is also called holy basil and has been used for centuries in India to reduce anxiety and stress. You can find both of them online or at a health food or natural grocery store.)

When I get back from dropping the kids off. With the breakfast dishes done (my husband tackles those while I drive the little people), I head for my home office/studio for yoga and meditation. When I first started meditating daily, I was fierce about my 20-minute sit each morning. But I think I had a lot of stress to detox. Now, in a pinch I actually go for the yoga over the sit because I know that my body has to move a little before I can sit comfortably anyway. If I can only do one, I make my yoga a kind of meditation and allow my mind to be gentle and relaxed and move through the poses slowly and steadily.

Nothing replaces the "clean slate" feeling in my mind after a 20-minute breath meditation though, so I still do one of those most days. Then, if the weather is nice, I enjoy breakfast in the front yard. (It is best not to do yoga/meditate on a full stomach.)

PRACTICE: Your Three Most Important Tasks (MITs)

When it's time to sit down at the desk, I write three things that must be done today on a sticky note. These are my MIT's or Most Important Tasks. It is important to do this after meditation and before I power up the computer or, God forbid, start emailing. I keep a bigger work-flow list but the sticky notes are nice because I can crumple them up and recycle when I'm done, which is strangely satisfying. Plus, they help me laser in.

It is not that you will only get three things done each day, but setting your own priorities and not reacting to life and email is very satisfying. Also, the MITs help you build a sense that you can trust yourself to name and live into those goals that are most important to you.

I hope this tour helps you think through your current morning routine and what might enliven it. Choose just one thing to incorporate (or to eliminate) and try it out for at least a week and observe the benefits, not just in your morning, but in your whole day.

PRACTICE: Identify Your Non-Negotiable Time (NNTs)

In addition to your morning routine, it is so helpful to infuse your day with a handful of activities that help you come home to yourself. You can enjoy these during breaks from work or before or after your workday. They are those simple things that just make you feel like you. These are non-negotiable if we want to create a life of impact that feels good to be in.

How do you normally show yourself kindness? I'm not talking about the self-care things you think you *should* do, but the gentle offerings you actually crave and enjoy. For me, three or more lovefest rubdowns with my kitty Beatrix, plus twenty minutes of meditation/yoga in the morning, lemon water and journaling are my current NNTs. These are somewhat seasonal and once spring comes, they will include at least five minutes gardening with my hands on something green. I also require at least one meal a day, preferably two, to be warm and home-cooked and eaten without any distractions.

Bringing It All Together: Sophie's Story

My coaching client Sophie is a mom of two lively kids, and a marketing entrepreneur. Her husband passed away a few years ago. Consequently, Sophie is acutely aware of how important it is each day for her to balance her own entrepreneurial and income-generating priorities with the needs of her family and her own need for self-care. She reached out for coaching support and we worked together to create her morning routine. Sophie explained that she felt totally off balance, a little lost and like she needed to establish a framework to guide her days. Some troubling things were also happening, including a devastating identity theft, a hit-and-run car accident and other negative energies that she felt swirling around her. For all of these reasons, she wanted to be super intentional about structuring her day in a way that supported her and her most precious priorities.

Sophie's NNTs need to flex every day. She said at first that she drove herself crazy trying to make them fit into a rigid routine which was the same day in and day out. Now, she has established a list of luscious options and she chooses one or more every morning and one or more before her work day wraps up and she picks up her children. These include a walk on a trail near her house, yoga, a power nap, a nourishing meal or snack and a guided meditation.

Checking in with her months later, she says that identifying a simple structure with time and space for regular centering practices has made a huge impact. Sophie explains: "Although each day doesn't start the same for me, what I did take away was that the practices we developed can and need to be inserted SOMEWHERE in my day to create the stability and security I need." Sophie provides a great example of a *custom* routine, balancing her need for flexibility with a container of regular support.

No matter how you design it, I hope your morning routine, MITs and NNTS give you some breathing room and make you more receptive to the pleasures both of work and of everyday life. Also remember that these are practices, not a quick fix. If you try them one day and the next day find yourself flying back into overwhelm, don't worry, simply observe how you feel and let yourself begin again.

These practices free up energy for contributions that are uniquely yours to make: your legacy work. That is beautiful and vital not just to *your* life and happiness but also to the story we are writing in this world together.

6 OVERCOME YOUR GREMLINS

Last night, I received an email with feedback about a retreat I was invited to lead for a local women's group. I called my husband in to read it. "Great job!" he said, getting ready to stand up and head back to finish the dinner dishes. Then he caught the look on my face and slowly lowered back into his chair.

There was a line in the email about how some participants criticized the retreat and didn't think that it matched what they were expecting. While the woman who crafted the email only referenced this "few" in her email to say how sad she thought it was that they were closed off to this material, my attention was completely hijacked by that one line. The thought that I could pour my heart, soul and mind into this event and still be evaluated as coming up short and, in particular, the knowledge that there was a small group behind the scenes discussing and criticizing my presentations? Excruciating.

As my husband watched the tears leak out of my eyes, he had his own look of despair. "I can't believe that is what you are focused on in this email!" he said. "She loved it!

She is effusive about how great the event was for her, one of the best she has ever been to!" "I know," I replied in a small voice. "I do see that what I'm giving attention to here is way off in terms of the whole ratio of the feedback. But that only makes it worse. Like what is wrong with me that I am so sensitive and can't drink in the good and instead only focus on the critique?"

We sat and talked for a few more minutes, me alternating between tears and ultimately laughing as I started teasing him saying, "You have your own version of crazy. You tend not to believe it when people say nice things about your work either!" And knowing that I was super tired – after the retreat I had also written the chapter on the Enneagram – I made the choice to close down the computer, take a shower and go to bed. This morning, the world looks quite a bit brighter.

But why is it that in certain contexts, the criticism of others can penetrate so deeply? That we can lose all sense of perspective or chase the approval even as our mind knows that exclusively positive feedback is an impossible goal? It is because, as we discussed previously, in relation to work envy, the problem doesn't really originate with other people. The criticism cuts because it hitches a ride on our own inner gremlins.

Defining Gremlins

"Gremlins" is a playful term to describe those painful or limiting thoughts that we have about ourselves. They are the voice of the inner critic. They dwell inside of us and they magnify the criticism of others until (on a bad day) the echo can fill up all the space inside. They steal our happiness and our ease and make us uncomfortable in our own lives. They are also one hundred percent human. No one is immune to gremlins.

The more we are able to move gremlins from the shadows of our attention, where they can be under the surface unconsciously driving us forward (and faster) through our lives and instead lift them to the surface, the more we can see them for what they are. Gremlins represent an interior judgment of reality (or of ourselves); they are not, in fact, the Ultimate Truth. Once we see that they are not reality itself we can employ simple tools to minimize our gremlins and in so doing find ever more freedom.

Like my client Amanda who shares: "One of the biggest gremlins I deal with is fear. Fear of the unknown, fear of failing (a big one), fear of missing out, fear of not measuring up, fear of disappointing someone (but that someone is rarely myself). Fear, fear, fear!" She deals with these gremlins by doing a gratitude meditation, acknowledging all the things she has accomplished and all the fear walls she has knocked down over the years.

When her fear is of failing at a task or a job, Amanda tries something that I recommend. She sets a timer to limit how long she is going to spend doing it. She reports that this makes it easier to try, knowing that she only has to do it for a certain amount of time. Other strategies Amanda finds helpful for dissolving gremlins: She calls a friend or family member to get a pep talk or just jumps right into the deep end of it, even if she is scared, knowing that she is smart and capable and brave and can handle anything that life throws at her.

Gremlins Put Your Nervous System on High Alert

Made famous by the 1980s movie of the same name, a gremlin is defined as "an imaginary mischievous sprite regarded as responsible for an unexplained problem or fault." The name may have derived from the word goblin and all of those resonances fit. This is a trickster, a prankster. And here is the dangerous thing. Gremlins can migrate. And once you start to criticize yourself for being critical, then you are really trapped.

For example, earlier this year, my friend Lynn came to visit. Together, she and I have six children. Whenever she visits, I usually feel like I'm living in the best version of my commune fantasies. (I've been around enough communities to know that living together with your friends/fellow seekers can go horribly wrong. But with certain dear friends, for short amounts of time, I can revel in a full house.)

Before she came, I had gotten in touch with a book coach and scheduled a free consultation. I kept waiting for the confirmation email with the details. They never showed up in my inbox but I was too distracted with hosting and long, lovely conversations to try and figure out what had gone wrong. Then the morning of the free coaching session arrives. My friend is packing up to leave that same day and the plan is that I hole up in my home office for this one hour while she loads the car and keeps an eye on the kids (Did I mention how many we have and how *very* loud all of them can be together?)

So, just a few minutes before the time for the scheduled call, I realize 1) I had missed the earlier confirmation email in spam and 2) I don't know how to use the phone/web service to connect with the coach, who is based in the UK. To make matters worse, I see her tweeting me and giving further instructions. In that moment, with the kids pounding at the office door, I couldn't even figure out how to tweet back from my computer. (Judge me if you must, Twitter is not my love language.) Aargh. I felt so lonely, like an astronaut who couldn't connect with her home base. I missed the interview and although I emailed her right then to apologize, of course I felt bad for wasting her time.

As I left the office, I had this urge to run away. Sitting with my friend in our final moments together, I had an excruciating sense that I was missing something else that was important. Yet, ignoring my guest right before she left town felt wrong too. It was all wrong. Later that day, I called my husband and grumbled about the email caught in the spam folder and the feeling of having reached a couple of rungs up the professional ladder to this book coach and then come across as less than professional. Ouch.

After an SOS text message to a couple of friends who are fellow coaches, I got a chance to talk it through with one of them who asked if there was a metaphor for how I felt about the situation. I said I had a sense of tripping and landing, kersplat. My insightful colleague said: "I have a hunch that you feel that you shouldn't have played. That you think you shouldn't have taken the whole week off to be with your friend and that your inner overachiever wouldn't have let this happen." What a wakeup call! My gremlins and overachiever impulses had migrated. I was on to them in regular life but now there they were perched around this book project, one of my juiciest new goals, like a row of vultures. Hi friends.

Gremlins put your nervous system on high alert. Scanning the horizon looking for threats, you might not realize that the noisy alarm shouting "Danger! Danger!" is actually coming from inside your own brain. It is coming from those internalized concerns and experiences that have rattled you in the past and still haunt you. Some people hear gremlins as audible voices driving them onward. For most of us, they are also accompanied by an internalized body pressure. Gremlins are always conditional, meaning they only evaluate you as being OK if some external standard is met; when others think well of you, for example, or when there is no tension in your surrounding circle or when you are in complete control of a situation.

When I asked my Facebook community for some current examples of gremlins, they shared freely. Here are my favorites.

Some gremlins can focus our attention on blaming others:

"He doesn't understand where I'm coming from; he never has and never will."

Others invite us to ignore our own needs for fear of how we will come across to others:

"You need to do more to help, your stuff can wait."

"If things fall apart, everyone will blame me."

Or they can keep us from really stretching ourselves to try something new:

"This is too hard. This should be easier, more intuitive."

Keep us locked in fear:

"What if I am missing the most amazing/important thing of my life?"

Or push us to try to influence or control a situation that is beyond our scope:

"Do not be weak. Shield up."

"You can't trust anyone, only depend on yourself."

Our Enneagram personality has a big influence over the gremlins that are loudest, but most of us can relate to housing a whole family of critical thoughts, which emerge at various times depending on the challenges we face. Whatever the flavor of the message, your gremlins ensure that you keep chasing a prize that you can never catch. Think of dogs chasing a bunny around the race track. Even if you could catch it, as quickly as you meet the gremlin's standard you realize that it's a plywood bunny wrapped in cotton fur. Fake food. It doesn't nourish you.

Sometimes, we don't hear the words so much as *feel* their effects, like a heaviness in the body. Depending on your Enneagram type, the emotions that accompany the gremlins most often could be a jangly anxiety (head types), a swamp of shame or sadness (heart types), or the familiar heat of anger or frustration (gut or body types).

For example, my client Rachel reports hearing the following gremlins: "If I take time for me, everything else won't get done. Or if I start working for myself, I'll never make enough money. I probably don't even have the basic skills to do this! It would be irresponsible to pursue this risky direction as a single mom." What helps her quiet the gremlins? In addition to meditation and thinking of inspiring examples of other women who have accomplished similar goals, she also likes to remind herself that she doesn't have to figure it all out overnight. So true!

Overcoming Your Gremlins

First, know that you aren't alone. Self-criticism has been a well-observed part of the human condition for millennia. So instead of judging yourself for judging yourself (oh, the irony), try rolling out the red carpet.

I like to tell my gremlins, "You can stay. It's fine. But I am going to feed you some good food." By which, I don't mean shoveling chocolate in my mouth, which is what the gremlins might think they want. Instead, I'm going to really nourish my body and enjoy some slow meals and slow conversations, both of which have a way of softening the gremlin voices and stretching my attention back out from the places where it has gotten painfully constricted. The gremlins can still be there and yet, in somehow accepting the wholeness of who we are, things start to shift.

Many of the busy women I work with are focused on others – being the good friend, lover, partner, and parent – as well as wanting to make their mark professionally and creatively by pursuing awards or opportunities for further development or accomplishment. Their gremlins keep the internal pressure high to succeed at *all* of it.

These interests and demands on their time keep women generating and giving long beyond the moment when their inner coffers are empty. This is when we start to cannibalize ourselves. We eat our own hearts, mental health and inner spaciousness in our desire to keep contributing "out there," which is how we can end up with lives that look good on the outside but don't actually *feel* good to be in.

When we are in this overproduction or overcompensation mode, one of the simplest methods we can use to reset our day and reestablish a relationship with ourselves is to practice the art of receiving.

I'll give you an example. This morning, I got up early to write. My writing mood yesterday afternoon had not been good, as I got lost in technical questions and research projects for other chapters. This stirred up some familiar gremlins: "I'm not going to finish. Even if I do finish this book is not really any good. It is not serving anyone."

Those are some of my main gremlin voices – especially a sense of scarcity around time and always feeling behind, like others are using rocket fuel to achieve their goals and I'm trudging up the mountain. Also, the feeling that whatever I have to offer is somehow deficient.

Luckily, the writing was flowing again this morning and I snuck in a good forty-five minutes in the studio before my little one came to get me. As I emerged with her into our kitchen, I was able to really see and better yet *receive* with all my senses the sweetness of the scene. My husband standing there, making oatmeal, and the smell of cinnamon and coffee in the air. Vintage Paul Simon floating out of the speaker. My children still in their pajamas and all soft around the edges, just waking up to the day.

I could have easily let that wash past me and stay attuned only to the gremlins and the list of things to do stretching before me. In fact, that is how our brains are hardwired. As Rick Hanson explains in his book *Hardwiring Happiness,* our brains are like sieves for the good experiences and Velcro for the bad.

But instead of letting the breakfast experience drain away, I really soaked it up. In addition to savoring the sights and smells of the morning, I took a few slow breaths, because this kind of receiving happens on a body plane as well as in the brain. It actually takes the body an average of eleven seconds to absorb a positive experience. Can you guess how quickly we take in negative energy? Half a second.

As I breathed in the goodness in front of me, I felt those tight places inside begin to melt and soften. My mood brightened. I felt reconnected to the life I am living now and how, in all its imperfection and my own, it fits me so very well. This certainly hasn't always been true for me; but that is exactly what these eight Flourish steps enable you to do. Working together, they engineer a sacred edit of your life equipping you to step-by-step crowd out what is no longer serving you and nurture the experiences that do.

But even if or when you get the externals lined up in way that feels good – at work, at home and in your community – you still will have to contend with gremlins. It is simply part of the experience of being human. We should take a cue from Elizabeth Gilbert, who explains in *Big Magic* that fear and doubt can be present in the life of the creative but they have to ride in the back seat.

And here is the super important thing to know: **Gremlins, our critical inner voices, actually get louder when we are growing.** This is so vital to understand because I have seen many clients confused by this phenomenon. As they stretch in a new direction in their work or in a relationship, the gremlins are seriously on the prowl and they read it as a warning sign that they are heading in the wrong direction. They say, "Oh, never mind. I'll just go back to the way I was."

Unfortunately, regardless of the fear, we can never really go back. The old order is simply not a fit anymore. It is like a child trying to put on the clothes from a younger year; it won't work no matter how much we try to squeeze in. What can happen is an experience of getting stuck – not feeling courageous enough to name what we really desire but deeply unsatisfied in our current situation. This is an awful space to live in. Which is why we need to equip ourselves to contend with gremlins so we can grow through them and receive that next level of our lives, which beckons to us. (To learn about my favorite body tool for overcoming gremlins – tapping, or acupressure – visit Chapter 7: Understand the Language of Your Body.)

Bringing it All Together: Morgan's Story

Morgan felt like she accidentally created a habitat for an entire family of gremlins to move into her life in the process of trying to reconnect to her creative self. When she was in her twenties, she left her graduate program in urban planning to get her MFA in encaustic painting. Living as an artist and surrounded by other artists was really fun for her but she couldn't, at that time, make it work as a profession, so she headed back into a career in city planning.

While she has had a wonderful career, it really took over a lot of her life. And although she feels that being part of a team designing cityscapes to benefit Denver residents is really creative in nature, it doesn't feel the same as those years when she was working exclusively as an artist. Now in her mid-forties, she is trying to regain some of the old painter in her, but feels that everything is rusty and tired, which has allowed this family of gremlins to move in.

Here is a little of what they have to say:

- You are too old to turn this around.
- You have lost it and you aren't getting it back.
- Everything you are painting now is crap and isn't worth your time or effort.
- You are too boring to create anything beautiful now.

Pretty grim voices, right? Do you feel compassion for Morgan, caught in this cascade of gremlins that limit her current life options? What would you say to her? How might you encourage her to look beyond these voices into a larger landscape? Perhaps you would remind her that she brings a whole wealth of life and professional experiences into her art now, which she didn't have before. Or that this isn't an all or nothing venture; she can create art *and* continue in her city planning work and find meaning in both. Whatever you might say to Morgan is *exactly* the kind of voice I want you to hold onto for yourself. Tap into that place of compassion and expansiveness the next time your gremlins pop up, let them know that it is fine for them to be there but don't let them steer your life.

Dissolving Your Gremlins

The fastest way to metabolize gremlins is by being kind to yourself even with those voices present. In fact, rather than running the other way, intentionally dive into those painful thoughts and dissolve them by gathering evidence that proves them wrong.

I'll give you an example. When I started my coaching business, my first client was a mom I knew in the neighborhood. What was challenging was that she didn't pay me when she had agreed to pay. I can remember the conversation I had with my sister at the time. She was trying to encourage me but I was wallowing in the gremlin voices and focused only on what was going wrong. I remember saying to her: "This isn't really going to work. I can't expect to regularly attract women who will invest in and value coaching." This is the trouble with gremlins. They don't report facts (though it can feel that way) but they add a whole other layer: *what we make the situation mean.*

So, my first client didn't pay me. Did that really mean that all was doomed? No. It had simply stirred up my insecurity regarding the viability of my new business and the value of my services as a coach. Eventually I was able to calm down my fears and get a little perspective on the situation. This allowed me to begin to think more creatively about my options and I started collecting payment *before* the session. I followed up with that first client, who eventually paid as well.

Then I was off...collecting more and more evidence that challenged those painful thoughts about unreliable clients as I worked with lovely women who paid on time, engaged their coaching journey with zest and followed through between sessions. Eventually, given all the data to the contrary, that particular set of gremlins just dissolved.

PRACTICE: Do "The Work"

When nothing else is helping and the critical voices remain, I love to take myself on a walk and engage in "The Work," a tool created by Byron Katie. I wish I had known about The Work when I was struggling with my first client. Let's imagine that you're starting your own business and are having the same problem. What do you do?

First, identify the central, painful thought that's troubling you. Say "They are never going to pay me." Now, ask yourself a series of questions about that thought: "Is it true?" "Can I one hundred percent know that it's true?" "How do I treat myself when I believe this thought?" For instance, maybe you tap into a place of needing to *push and prove* your worth—out of fear of not being perceived as valuable. Then ask, "How do I treat other people when I believe in this thought?" Maybe you turn with a suspicious gaze to prospective clients, wondering who next will flake out. Not a very appealing posture for new clients, right?! See how these painful thoughts can really shape and limit our lived experience?

Finally ask yourself, "Who would I be without this thought?" For example, imagine that you wake up and everything is the same in your life except you're unable to think this thought. Maybe you would feel free to simply be in the learning phase of building a new business, without attaching so much meaning to any one interaction. (These questions are adapted from The Work by Byron Katie. To learn more, visit www.thework.com.)

You may prefer to answer these questions in a journal, staying in a calm, reflective state. Now that I've done The Work for several years, I've internalized the questions and prefer to get outside and get moving, exploring the painful thought while I walk. However you do it, answering these questions is often enough to defang the gremlin and drain the painful thought of its sting, so that you can continue growing forward.

7 UNDERSTAND THE LANGUAGE OF YOUR BODY

"You do not have to be good.
You do not have to walk on your knees
for a hundred miles through the desert, repenting.
You only have to let the soft animal of
your body love what it loves."
— Mary Oliver "Wild Geese"

I used to live in constant fear of a body breakdown. Recurrent migraines and bladder infections were a big part of my story starting in my early twenties and continuing off and on for almost two decades. Worse than the symptoms themselves was the feeling that I was somehow defective. I had gotten a broken body, a dysfunctional body. I was overly sensitive to life's stresses and didn't have the resiliency that others seemed to enjoy.

When I would come down with one of my regular symptoms or with a cold, flu, or sinus infection, I would feel like a failure. Like I was letting down the people I worked with or for; like the time spent recuperating was wasteful and distancing me from my tightly held goals.

I would also fear getting sick. "What if I agree to teach at this event and end up with a UTI?" I felt like I didn't have the fuel that I needed for the fire I wanted to build through my work.

Can you relate? How do you treat yourself when you are sick? Can you let yourself lay down your obligations and truly heal or do you find yourself limping along at half speed until your symptoms morph into something so painful or serious that they require total submission (like the migraine that forces you to close your curtains and do nothing but lay still in bed)? Or maybe you don't worry about getting sick before a big event but instead find yourself routinely crashing once the work is done?

Your Animal Body

Ah, bodies. We cannot ignore this gorgeous vessel we inhabit. However, many of my clients don't trust it. They see their body as something that needs to be managed instead of something that can be enjoyed – a means to an end, like the vehicle that carries them through life toward their goals.

I totally get it.

I remember a day that captures so perfectly my old habit of relating to my body. I was walking along the Charles River in Cambridge and crossed a bridge by the Harvard boathouse. On the bridge, I encountered a seal that said, in Latin, something like Mind, Body, Spirit.

And I got pissed. Here I was pushing and stretching myself in these two competitive graduate programs (which honestly didn't play nicely together – I had whiplash moving between the Harvard Divinity and Kennedy Schools) and it felt like this centuries-old seal was taunting me.

"The people who study here are the best of the best," it whispered. "To measure up, you need to be fully educated academically, have a robust spiritual life and be totally fit." "Well, that is just wonderful," I thought. "Exactly what I need. More pressure." I knew I could hold my own in the intellectual department (with plenty of hours at the library) and I knew that I had gifts and passions in the spiritual domain but the *body*?!

I'm sure it didn't happen this way in real life, but in my memory, this inner dialogue was punctuated at that exact moment by taut, gorgeously-limbed rowers passing under the bridge, every muscle flexing and moving in unison, not an extra ounce of fat on anyone's body.

Fabulous.

This was the only way I could imagine relating to my body and "succeeding" at it: if I had some amazingly fit physique or was a super star athlete. Those were so not in the realm of the possible for me. Well, I suppose the fabulous fit physique *could* have been possible, but I never unlocked the code to eating less and exercising religiously, which might have given me such a body.

As for being an athlete, that was clearly out of the question. I was on a soccer team when I was five and it had honestly terrified me. I am terrible at volleyball and mediocre at kickball, though I have tried at many a beach barbeque, only to feel my cheeks redden at how totally uncoordinated I am. Nearly any sport I've been required to play in school or socially pressured to play since then can send me into a shame spiral.

By this time on the bridge, though, I had discovered a few body practices that I genuinely enjoyed. In college, I took a class that helped me strengthen my swimming and I came to enjoy doing laps. I also took a weight training program for women my senior year (because I needed a final PE/wellness credit) and ended up enjoying it. This class of women would all come into the weight room and capture it from the sweaty males, who would vacate the scene. Together, we got comfortable learning how to work the machines and track our progress.

Then in the Peace Corps, I discovered how much I love hiking, as the mountainous terrain in Nicaragua required it. And I've always loved dancing, especially in my socks in the living room. But none of these practices would put me anywhere close to "excelling" in my body by some external standard.

What I didn't know in that moment on the bridge – about eighteen months before I would have my first child – was how much childbirth would offer me a whole new way to relate to my body.

The birth of our son Coleman didn't go as planned. I had envisioned a beautiful, peaceful homebirth and instead we needed to transfer to the hospital. I felt such a sense of dismay and failure that the whole thing did not unfold as I had hoped.

Yet, when I look back on that experience ten years later, I actually see it as the dawn of my interest in and awareness of the mind-body connection. Childbirth was not something I could will or perform my way through. Instead, it invited me to trust my body's wisdom and look honestly at the painful gremlins that come up in my self-talk around it. These lessons equipped me for very different experiences with the births of my two daughters, one at a birth center and the other at home.

I am so grateful for all that I learned through these births, especially the power of kindness and how relating to my body with compassion and gentleness – instead of barking at it like a drill sergeant for disappointing me – is actually what opens the door for serious health improvements and body resiliency.

Now, your body may have performed much better for you. You may excel at sports or birth babies with ease. But if there is any inner harshness about the way you relate to your animal body, this chapter is for you.

Your Body Compass

Why go to the trouble of learning to speak the language of your body? At the end of the day, what do you gain? Your body is one of your most potent allies in moving through the changes you desire.

In addition to helping you identify where and how you are holding stress, your body sensations also operate as a kind of compass that you can read to discern the next best steps for your life. At its simplest, the language of the body is expansion or contraction. Our body feels light and open when we are pointed in a direction that jibes with our true nature or essential self. It feels contracted or closed when we are heading away from such a choice or in the direction of something that doesn't fit us.

As Martha Beck explains in *Finding Your Own North Star*, if we can learn to listen through the static of our minds and the "shoulds" of our social selves in order to attend to this body compass, it can produce some really dramatic results. For example, consider the last time you overrode your "gut" feeling about something because your head talked you into it. How did that turn out?

Still feeling skeptical? Not a problem. This tool is designed to be explored in real life, which will always be your best teacher. The body compass only gets stronger and suppler the more we use it.

You may be someone who is already attending to your body cues. If so, that's fantastic. This chapter will help you turn up the volume on your body channel even more. If you tend to feel out of touch with your body, this chapter provides several simple, effective strategies for re-connecting.

If you have some major decisions to make – around changing jobs or leaving a relationship – you may feel lost in competing thoughts and unsure which direction to take. Utilizing your body compass is the best way to know when it's time to make a move. Communication with the body is the foundation for trusting yourself.

4 Ways to Speak the Language of Your Body

Strategy 1: Identify Your Stress Response

I have a friend who is going through a growth spurt. She is upping her game in her coaching business and life and is feeling more "seen" in the world after spending several years at home with her girls. We talked recently and I offered some cheerleading and laser coaching to help her gain traction on moving through some of her current obstacles. When we wrapped up the call, we both admitted how much more fun it is to get to be the coach than to be the one who is stretching, hurting, growing or otherwise stirred up. But each of us also recognized how much our own willingness to stay present with ourselves and to observe our process when we are stressed or struggling is completely central to our authenticity and our capacity as a coach.

No one gets to push the "spiritual bypass button" and completely avoid being rattled. Or if they seem to, they might just be pretending. We don't get to choose when our stress response is triggered any more than we can prevent emotional or physical pain. Our fight or flight response can be tripped by an external circumstance – for example, a mean email – or an internal one – what we make the email mean, i.e. "I'm going to lose my job," or "I screwed this up and now others will think less of me."

Little did I realize how soon after this phone call that my turn would come. I was feeling centered and happy with wisdom to share one minute and humble and shaky the next. I know no way off of this human ride but offer here a case study for how to identify your stress response so that you can reset as quickly and as painlessly as possible.

A few hours after my conversation with my friend, I was in a slightly euphoric state because of the near completion of my kitchen remodel (and likely the paint fumes) and settled down to get caught up on a flurry of emails that were related to a volunteer project I led at our school garden.

And I was email sniped. You know what this is: when someone sends you a message that is snarky, mean-spirited or otherwise implying something less than good about you / your choice / leadership / work, etc. I felt unjustly blamed and pissed.

I'm rather conflict-avoidant but I like to spearhead and organize community projects. So, I end up with an interior struggle between the part of me that naturally takes the lead and the part that's shaking in her boots in the face of others' opinions. In fact, these parts of my personality live in perpetual creative tension. I get that leaders are never going to be met with a one hundred percent approval rating. My head understands this and, yet, I get all stirred up when conflict emerges or when someone questions my choices.

This email (and the underlying stressors in my life) triggers my stress response. In the moment, I freeze. Literally, as I take in the surprise email, I can feel myself sort of gulp air and a protective layer drop over the front of my heart. Then, I start the blame game. Often our stress response feels like a strong reaction to another person. The anger can be a clue that boundaries need to be set or reset.

But the stress response itself is happening within *your* body.

The fight or flight response spikes our cortisol, a stress hormone, which generates a whole host of fallouts. It makes our breath shallower, raises our blood sugar and shifts the blood away from lovely regenerative things like resting, digesting or even spacious thinking and pumps it to the muscles so you can actually run away or fight the damn thing.

"Freeze" is actually the lesser known component of the stress response. It's what you do when you feel like you can't fight or flee and is akin to playing dead. Think of the gazelle in the lion's jaws being dragged away. If it plays dead, there is a slim chance that the lion will deposit its meal and go somewhere else, thus allowing the stunned antelope to escape. It's a long shot, which is why it is the body's last-ditch effort.

Depending on your personality type, you may be more likely to fight, flee or freeze in the face of perceived danger. That is a helpful question to ask yourself. For example, the personality I lead with – Type Three, the performer or organizer – has a habit of freezing in the heart when in the line of fire or feeling overwhelmed. Your impulse may be to fight or make a run for it.

Equally important is to understand how your stress response feels in *your* body. For me, in addition to the numbness in my chest, cold hands and rapid breathing are further clues. Clients identify a whole range of different feelings when their stress mounts. Some are inclined to eat or overeat to push down the negative emotions; others find themselves getting more aggressive – energetically pushing their agenda forward – while others tend to retreat or disappear, or experience racing thoughts like being on trial in their minds.

We all experience a whole range of symptoms but one or two will be the strongest indicators that *your* fight / flight / freeze response has been activated. See if you can identify them. These will then be your clues to engage some hands-on mind-body tools, what I call your DIY Stress Reduction Formula.

Now, back to my email situation. I have a little bit of an edge around being a touchy-feely person. In fact, I really resent when people assume that I'm a pushover or weak because I'm emotive. I want to shout, "This is what feminine leadership looks like, people!" You don't have to lord power over others, boss them around or otherwise suck up all the oxygen in the room to initiate a change. You can, in fact, create lovely containers and structures for groups to shine.

With the right degree of accountability and elegant design (and some basic good will and tenacity), people in groups do things they never thought they could do. And honestly, they also do things that they couldn't have done alone. Like create a thriving school garden for hundreds of children, educators and families to enjoy. This form of power relies more on the art of collaborating and drawing goodness out of people for common benefit rather than strong-arming.

Yet, there always comes a point – and this has happened to me so many times I see it coming now – when there is a bully or unbounded person and, if I don't stand up to them, the balance in the group gets all out of whack. Taking the heat of conflict is really scary for me. My amygdala (the brain's smoke detector, which shouts "danger") is on high alert when these situations unfold and I would really rather run and hide. It is only my love for the change we are trying to create, in this case a garden/outdoor classroom, that inspires me to stand my ground.

It is also important to mention that when I received the email I had just completed a cleanse and was on a detoxifying diet with some unpleasant symptoms: headaches and just feeling a little green around the gills. Also, my kitchen had been barely functional for the previous month while we renovated. In fact, the night the email came in, my kitchen table was piled high with everything disgorged from my cabinets.

These details are relevant. The next time you get hijacked by your body's stress response, chances are that it won't just be one thing but rather many stressors, layered over time, that leave your bandwidth taxed. This is going to happen – it's part of life – and it is why I focus so much of my coaching and teaching on practices that boost resiliency, which is our capacity for absorbing and responding generously to life's bumps. Thankfully, these same practices also help us come back home to ourselves and our senses when our stress response has been tripped.

Now, if you are in a super busy or stressful season of life, you may feel like you are simply pinging from stress reaction to stress reaction with little downtime in between. I have completely been there. These same tools will also create a respite for you from that chronic stress state, which is necessary to discern what changes you need to make in your work and life in order to reduce your overall stress load.

Strategy 2: DIY Your Stress Reduction Formula

So how did I handle the email sniper? First, I got some quick support from my husband and garden co-chair to help me discern the next best steps. I responded in a brief email, took care of the concern she raised and made a note to better clarify our respective roles going forward. In that moment, I knew it was about doing the minimum to move the whole project forward and then turning my attention to myself and my own needs.

Nonetheless, I had a running monologue with this person in my head for the next few hours explaining my choices, defending our garden budget and on and on. I also noticed (the 5% of me that wasn't completely high-jacked by this stress reaction) that time had this different quality. Rather than the evening unfolding in its regular flow, it felt choppy. I would sort of "wake up" and discover that my tea, which I thought would still be warm, had grown cold while I was lost in a reverie. All night, regardless of what else I was doing, I had an extra script running on the side, arguing with someone in my head.

Attempting to move through regular life while caught in our fight / flight / freeze response is taxing. Instead, do something to move the stress out of your tissues first – like go for a brisk walk – or try tapping, my favorite hands-on tool for decreasing the stress load in the body, described in detail below.

PRACTICE: Tapping or Acupressure

Tapping combines ancient Chinese medicine with the contemporary fields of psychology and somatic (body) awareness. It is a concrete way to be sweet to your brain. Honestly, the brain can't help itself. It is high on mood-altering substances like your stress hormone cortisol, which make it laser in on the perceived threat. All those arguments you have in your mind with your boss or foe, whoever they may be, aren't really productive. You can recognize them for what they are – symptoms of the stress response – and choose to resource yourself with some tapping to quell your nerves.

This is the most powerful mind-body tool for immediate relief that I know. Whether your anxiety is sky-high, you are in real physical or emotional pain or just feel roughed up by life, tapping is always available to you. (I've been known to sneak to the bathroom to tap when I'm out in the world and face an unexpected challenge.) It is very easy. There are nine acupressure points on the head and the upper chest on which you can tap. (See the diagram on the next page.)

TAPPING POINTS

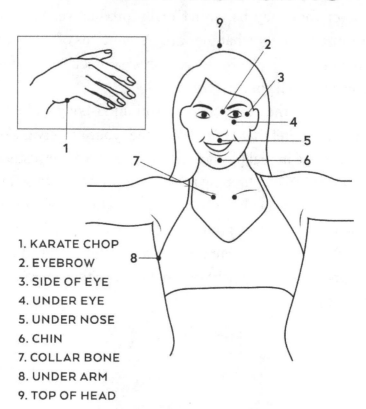

1. KARATE CHOP
2. EYEBROW
3. SIDE OF EYE
4. UNDER EYE
5. UNDER NOSE
6. CHIN
7. COLLAR BONE
8. UNDER ARM
9. TOP OF HEAD

This practice (think acupuncture minus the needles) is a simple, painless and highly effective way to defuse the emotional charge around a situation. Tapping sends a calming message to your amygdala – the almond-shaped structure in the brain that is responsible for detecting fear and preparing for emergency events. Part of the limbic or emotional system, the amygdala is also responsible for determining what and where memories are stored in the brain, thus influencing how large (or small) an emotional response will be evoked by future similar experiences.

Tapping on the acupressure points while running through painful or scary thoughts actually helps restore the whole nervous system and the balance of energy in the body. In effect, tapping defangs those painful thoughts – so you don't trip your own stress response the next time they come up – and rewires your brain to respond in fresh ways to the challenge.

How to Tap

First, you have to name the issue that you would like to defuse. Rank how strong this struggle is for you right now. How much is it bothering you on a scale of 1 to 10 (one being barely at all, ten being you didn't sleep at all last night or are in serious physical pain)? For example, if I had chosen to tap right after receiving that email sniper, I would have ranked my frustration at a six or seven out of ten.

Next, tap on the "karate chop point" on the side of your hand as you say three times: "Even though I [name the problem], I love and accept myself." Or if that feels too cheesy, try saying "Even though I [name the problem], I am ready to let it go." So, I might have said, "Even though I received this mean email about the garden and I am feeling really pissed, I love and accept myself." This statement sets up our tapping session and grounds it in the truth – not what we wish was happening but how we actually feel.

Now is your chance to stimulate and soothe your body's energy and begin to de-stress. Starting from the eyebrow point and moving in the order the acupressure points appear on the diagram, tap about 5 to 7 times on each point. Tap firmly like you are playing a drum. You don't want to hurt yourself; nor do you want to tap too lightly.

After tapping the underarm point (on the side of the body, usually where a woman's bra strap is), complete the tapping cycle at the crown point on the very top of your head. While you are tapping, name what is troubling you as if you were talking to a friend. Consider this your opportunity for "conscious complaining" – really let the truth of how you feel about a situation come out.

I might have said "This is totally unfair! I try really hard in this volunteer role and this is what I get! Why can't she see that what we request in our budget is for the good of the school garden and its future!" etc. Sometimes people don't want to give voice to their feelings, considering them petty or not wanting to "reinforce the negative." The truth is that running from how we actually feel only drives the feelings in deeper. Consider this your invitation to air out a challenge and actually voice those thoughts looping through your head *out loud*.

It is not necessary to tap on both sides of the body and okay to alternate from one side to another (our energy meridians run on both sides). Using two fingers to tap seems to increase the chances of targeting the exact point.

Move around, tapping all nine points and saying out loud what troubles you (hearing your own voice is important and will make the process more powerful). After you have finished two rounds, check in on the intensity of the problem and again rate it on a scale of one to ten. If the problem has reduced in intensity – yay! – do more rounds of tapping, adjusting the wording appropriately until you are satisfied or ready to move on.

Sometimes, the issue morphs while you tap or, in the case of a physical pain, it moves elsewhere in the body. In the latter case, you just need to continue tapping and naming what is true for you currently as your experience shifts. For example, my anger at the garden email might dissolve into sadness at the pain of being misunderstood or feeling undervalued. If so, I just continue to tap now on the new feelings. Occasionally, the issue even increases in intensity. This is powerful feedback for you that you are on a "hot track" with your tapping and really starting to shift and defuse some old energy. If the feelings get stronger, simply take a breath, adjust your wording to fit what you currently feeling and are keep tapping!

At whatever point you start to feel some relief or are ready to move on with your day, it can also be beneficial to tap a "positive" round or two to express the positive emotions or sense of new possibilities that you have discovered. For example, once I started to feel better, I might continue tapping a round and say things like "Maybe this garden situation will not feel so intense tomorrow. I know that I can trust myself to speak up for what I think is true and I am strong enough to be open to others' perspectives."

You don't have to get to a zero every time – even a shift of a few numbers down the scale is huge! That could be the difference between 1) a conflict hijacking your attention all day long and 2) the same conflict slipping into the background, allowing you to attend to your own priorities and deal with it later, as needed. Or the difference between a level of physical pain that puts you in bed and one that is manageable enough to allow you to engage (slowly and mindfully) in your regular routine.

Again and again, I find that tapping enhances my quality of life and helps me find a path forward. It can feel a bit complicated at first but is super easy once you get the hang of it. Tapping in the shower at the end of the day is one of my favorite ways to clear out any residue before bed.

Also, if I go to sit for a session of meditation and find the thoughts won't let me rest and I'm caught up arguing with someone in my mind, that is another good time for me to tap. Occasionally, I'll even spend the whole twenty minutes of meditation tapping if I am really struggling. Also, I sometimes like to tap for five minutes when I sit at my desk before I start the work day. Play with it – make this practice your own.

For a quick video that will help you find your acupressure points and show you how to tap, look in your Flourish Kit, a collection of free gifts for readers at www.courtneypinkerton.com/flourishkit.

PRACTICE: Additional DIY Stress Reduction Tips

In addition to tapping, light exercise is also super helpful when you are trying to de-stress. Heavy exercise can actually trigger your fight or flight further so you want to get moving but keep the intensity down. Consider walking or yoga or other gentle exercises to discharge that extra stress from your body.

Also, if you have access to a bathtub, a regular detoxifying bath with Epsom salt and your favorite essential oils is a powerful stress response reset. Even without the tub, you can enjoy the oils with a diffuser. Lavender is a perennial favorite for calming nerves, wild orange oil also reduces anxiety and boosts your mood, geranium oil is nourishing for the heart and frankincense is both grounding and great for your skin. I don't recommend you put peppermint oil in the bath (it has that icy hot feeling, especially if it gets into sinuses or sensitive places), but it is a great mind and sinuses clarifier and a wonderful pick me up in the afternoon to diffuse or smell directly out of the bottle.

If you would like more information about essential oils, I created a quick reference guide of my top ten favorite essential oils and how to use them. You will find it in the Flourish Kit at www.courtneypinkerton.com/flourishkit.

Strategy 3: Reintroduce Yourself to Your Body

At the time that I had my frustration on the bridge at Harvard, I was very disconnected from my body. Far from being an expert on the mind-body connection, I was actually an expert in how to *override* my body's signals to continue down the path I was intent on travelling. You can burn your body's energy this way for a while, especially when you are young or if you rely heavily on caffeine, sleeping pills and others substances to drive your body's energy up and down.

But if you really want to establish a life that you enjoy, this requires noticing the subtle signals that emerge from the body plane. This is not *thinking* about the body so much as it is about *sensing* the body. For most of us, it is a bit of a shift.

Body sensations include things like:

- hunger
- a full bladder
- tight shoulders
- pain or constriction anywhere in the body
- sexual desire
- the felt sense of your breath
- sore muscles
- feet that hurt from uncomfortable shoes
- cold hands (or other sensations of cold or warmth elsewhere in the body)
- shaking after a stressful encounter
- relaxation felt in your body (like the release of energy you feel after you complete a big project)

These sensations are a wonderful gift because they invite us out of our heads (where we can be distracted by 50,000+ thoughts every day) and into the present moment, where our body lives.

Now your head, body and emotions can interact together in some interesting and confusing ways. In fact, your thoughts can *generate* an emotional response and concurrent body tension. But for now, we are focusing on the body sensations, regardless of what has caused them.

For some of my clients, syncing up with their body sensations can prove to be a real challenge, especially in the beginning. For years, they have relied only on their head or mental capacities to drive them and have tried to bypass their physical reality and body limits. Others struggle with perfectionism, wanting to *control* their bodies. If these ring true for you too, you can start building a new relationship with your body by engaging one of the practices described below. Also, please remember that reading about an exercise and doing it are two very different things, so I encourage you to put the book down, engage one of these and see how you feel afterward. Has anything shifted?

PRACTICE: The Deepest Breath You Have Had Today

Where do you feel your breath the strongest? Perhaps it is in the rise and fall of your belly, or in the back of your throat or in the coolness and warmth of the inhale and exhale at the tip of your nose. See if you can drop out of the habit of *thinking* about your experience and attend to your sensations in this moment. Take the deepest breath you have taken all day and allow a nice, slow exhale. Repeat four or five times and continue observing where you feel the breath in your body. Allow fresh oxygen and energy in with each inhale and release anything that is stale or that no longer serves you with each exhale.

As women, we can focus a lot of attention on the front of the body: hair, makeup, smiling and making social connections. If I need a reset, I like to take a few moments to breathe fully so that my rib cage expands in all directions and I can even feel my breath in my back. This is about reconnecting to my *whole body,* not just the part I can see in the mirror. Try it now and observe your experience.

PRACTICE: Your Body Timer

Another tip I find helpful is to set a reminder on your phone for a few times a day, like at 10:00 am, 2:00 pm and 7:00 pm. Each time it pings, simply drop in and notice, with compassion and curiosity, what is happening in your body at that moment.

Maybe you discover that you got really caught up in email and are actually thirsty. Could you get up and make yourself some nice lemon water? Or you find that your shoulders have crept up to your ears as you listen to the news and fill the dishwasher. Use the timer to remind you to stretch and readjust your posture. Could you enjoy some silence and a few standing yoga moves before you start your next activity?

You can even keep a journal about it for a few days. Become your own body detective. As you turn up the volume on these sensations by bringing your attention to them (remember what we pay attention to grows), you will be able to discern body cues more easily.

PRACTICE: Subversive Napping

It can be hard to discern those subtle body messages when you are fatigued. In fact, many of my clients don't even realize at first how tired they are. As they move through the Flourish Formula and begin to experiment with different practices, they discover that they can't meditate because they tend to just fall asleep.

Often, a nap is your next best step. I just took one myself after lunch. A twenty-minute daily nap is a wonderful gift to offer yourself. It can feel delicious and subversive. Don't work from home? No problem. Can you lock the door of your office, head to your car or find another space to put up your feet?

When I was in my final year of graduate school, had a toddler and was pregnant, I was able to use a special lounge to take a quick nap every day. It was a room they reserved for parents with infants and related needs. I remember emerging from my secret room feeling refreshed as I headed into the crush of fellow students moving between classes. Looking into my fellow students' faces, I felt like we all could have used a nap. Sometimes, it's simply a matter of asking for what you need.

However, a nap may not fit your lifestyle or the environment where you work. In that case, and truly for all of us, it is vital that you pay attention to how much you sleep at night. If the idea of getting eight to nine hours every night (you have to watch your own cues here, I'm really more of a 9-hour a night kind of person) feels overwhelming, see if you can tweak your schedule just by fifteen minutes.

For example, are you usually in bed at 10:45 pm? Can you try for 10:30 pm? Do that for a few days and observe what, if anything, shifts for you. In an ideal world, we all wake up without an alarm. That may not feel realistic at this point, but the amount of resistance you feel when it goes off is an important clue. If you have to peel your eyes open and stumble towards coffee day in and day out, your body might be trying to get your attention.

Lastly, if the idea of enjoying a nap or heading to bed earlier feels incredibly self-indulgent, this is a good clue that you may be harboring some gremlins that push you forward at an unsustainable pace. See if you can get clear on what these inner voices are saying and try tapping (a practice described earlier in this chapter) to diffuse them.

PRACTICE: Feel Your Hunger

In addition to breathing, setting a timer and napping, there is one other important tool for speaking your body's love language: remembering to eat when you are hungry and stopping when you are full. I would put this in the simple but not easy department for many busy women. If you have a hunger scale that runs from a negative ten to a positive ten (negative ten being the hungriest you have ever been and positive ten the most uncomfortably full), try to keep hunger between a -2 and + 2. If you are a little bit hungry, eat something. If you are a little bit full, stop. Eat away from your desk, outside in the fresh air if you can swing it. Warm lunches on my front porch are a big part of my daily body kindness formula or NNT (Non-Negotiable Time), which we talked about back in Chapter 5.

Exquisite Self-Care

If any part of you is under-impressed with these simple measures, I would simply encourage you to try incorporating some into your day – especially when you feel depleted or stressed out – and see if they shift anything for you. There is a world of difference between knowing about a body care practice and taking the time to first notice when you are struggling and to offer yourself some custom support. I call this approach *exquisite self-care*. It goes beyond the basics, like brushing your teeth, to really care for your deeper needs.

In addition to DIY reset measures, you may be experiencing some current or chronic health challenges that require you to be under a doctor's care. Or maybe you simply wish to improve your health baseline to enjoy more energy and a more resilient immune system. This is where involving other highly skilled body practitioners can be so worth the investment.

Strategy 4: Be the CEO of Your Own Wellbeing

My husband sometimes laughs at the team of body care practitioners I require. Some people are more stress-hardy naturally but that is not my story. To work and create at a level that matches my ambition and my desire to be of service, I require a carefully curated care team, which includes:

- a gifted yoga teacher
- two acupuncturists (one does muscle testing, the other is a master of Chinese herbs)
- a chiropractor
- a DO for basic health needs and physicals
- a holistic dentist
- a holistic OB/GYN

You may require a completely different web of support. Some people are motivated to research and find the modalities that best fit them. Others prefer a more organic approach of trial and error. Some practitioners do hands-on body work (like chiropractors, massage therapists and acupuncturists). Others work with you to care for your body and listen to it, like the naturopath who recommends a nutrition change and other "lifestyle medicine" strategies. Both working on and with the body are wonderful options; it simply depends on your comfort level and preferences. (I recommend Rachel Carlton Abram's *BodyWise* for more on working directly with your body's intelligence.)

At this point, I don't view my body as the weak link or wait for it to betray me with illness. Instead, I see it more as a partner. The chronic symptoms I experienced for years, while not completely gone, are now much better managed. When they do show up, I view them as messengers, as ways that my body communicates to keep me "between the rails" of my natural limits. And with easy DIY mind-body tools like tapping, plus the expert help of my wellbeing team, I feel so much more resourced when I need to reset from stress or heal.

This kind of relationship with your body, which is characterized by trust and ease, is absolutely possible and is what I hope for you. By slowing down, attending to body cues, upping awareness of the stress response and equipping yourself with DIY tools like tapping plus expert holistic care, you and your body can come to speak the same language. This coming together or "syncing up" of you with your body provides a foundation of health that enables you to flourish in mind, spirit *and* body.

Bringing it All Together: Cara's Story

Cara is a busy nonprofit executive with a husband who travels a lot for work and two little boys. She has recently been navigating a big professional move that would open up more of the kind of work that she wants to do (hands-on outreach with low-income communities). This move will require them to sell their house and relocate. While Cara is feeling a great deal of peace about the way this new opportunity is unfolding, she also feels a lot of pressure, especially about the number of changes that her boys will have to navigate.

During this time of transition, she started to feel some tension in her lower back. On a recent coaching call, she explained that before we started working together she would have ignored the growing back pain and simply been mad when she woke up one morning unable to move. Now she recognizes that the back pain is there and knows that it is related to the extra dose of stress in her current life circumstances.

Rather than being frustrated with herself (why can't I be less stressed?), Cara has learned to pay attention to what these body cues have to teach her. No longer needing the tension to evaporate, she makes space for it. She even gets curious about it. She also tries to take practical measures to support herself by doing yoga at home and not only at the studio, sitting on cushions to support her back and more.

When I asked her what her back would say if it could talk to her, she replied, "I'm moving too fast. Lifting and carrying too much. I can't carry it all by myself. I need to continue to find ways to ask for help."

As we talked more about how to ask for help, she realized that things were actually in pretty good shape with the house and the move preparations. She came to see that the thing she really needed more than anything else was to make space to play with her boys every day, to go on a bike ride or to play a game outside. She realized her back pain was reminding her to incorporate more fun and to discharge some of that extra tension with physical movement. In so doing, she modeled for her children a lesson that will benefit them well into the future: how to continue to *enjoy* your life even in times of transition and change.

8 RESET WITH MEDITATION

For many of us, meditation becomes one of those things that we feel we *should* be doing. As if, in addition to crafting meaningful contributions to the world and raising our kids or fur babies, we also need to be getting up at 5:00 am and heading to a tree house for sunrise yoga with green tea and our morning sit. First, that is not the only way to meditate; second, you can totally do this, even if you have tried before and felt like you failed.

There is no failure in meditation. It is simply a detox for your nervous system. So, I want to invite you to let go of your previous experiences and be willing to play around here. I know we can find a practice that is just right for you.

Defining Meditation: It Is Not What You Think It Is

One of the things that most surprises my clients is the discovery that when we are going through a growth spurt, the centering practices that we have relied on in the past often stop working. Far from being a bad thing, this is in fact evidence that you are evolving! It can feel kind of cruel though, to be going through a stretching time at work or in your personal life and to reach for that thing that has always made you feel better. Maybe you journal, or light candles, go for a long run or say a prayer in the shower, only to discover that it doesn't really seem to be helping you the way it used to.

Our spiritual practices are dynamic. They change over time as our needs change and as we move through different life phases. So please let them. And trust that you can find one or more practices in this chapter that are a good fit for you in this season of life. When it is time to let that go and try something else, you will know.

But there is a commitment worth making here. I spent years doing lots of meditation-like things whenever I felt like it. It was only six years ago, when I heard an interview with author and meditation teacher Sarah McClean in which she talked about the difference between life before and after a regular practice, that I decided to commit to daily meditation. (See *Soul Centered: Transform Your Life in 8 Weeks with Meditation* by Sarah McLean.) Honestly, I had spent years feeling like an overly-sensitive heart balloon, battered this way and that by the strong winds that were blowing in my life. Meditation helps me quell my nerves and feel more resourced from within. Think of it not as something you *do* so much as something you *drink*, a nourishing tonic for your nervous system.

My simplest description of meditation is probably not what you expect: no crossed legs required. Meditation is literally *anything* that helps you "go receptive." That is right. Any practice that helps you peel those little control-loving fingers off of your life and open back up to the fuller picture. Any practice that helps you remember you are not the one calling all the shots. Any practice that lets you drink in support, whether that support comes from tapping into God/Source, from the reminder that your breath is gorgeously moving (without you even having to do anything) or from the feeling of the ground beneath your feet or the nature outside your window. It could be a formal sit or it could be starting the day with your morning coffee outside, listening to the birds. My point is that you have choices here.

Why Meditate? Shilyh's Story

The best way for me to explain the benefits of meditation is to tell you about one of my meditation students. Shilyh is a film professor and the mother of two boys. Before starting her regular meditation practice, she felt like she couldn't quite keep up, even with herself. She says she was always operating at a high frequency, fast and sharp. And she felt that intensity especially in her family life, where she didn't have the bandwidth to enjoy and be present to the people around her. Her life had become an experience of giving too much at work and feeling that she was going too fast all the time.

Her husband saw a flyer about an eight-week meditation series that I was teaching and suggested it to her. Looking back on that interaction now, Shilyh says she can really feel the compassion that motivated her husband, how he saw her struggling and thought that meditation might bring the relief that she wanted but didn't know how to find by herself.

When she started meditating in the class she could feel the effects right away. It gave her a sense that another frequency was possible, that this "lower gear" was available to her. "I had it within me," she explains. "It was right here, I just forget to access it." Meditation opened the pathway for her to find that resource within herself.

Reflecting on the experience now, a few years later, Shilyh is really clear that the benefits of meditation are twofold. Not only does connecting to that slower speed during her ten-minute daily practice bring relief; another benefit is simply knowing that there is *something* she can offer herself when she starts to feel overwhelmed that she is confident will help change her mood or pace.

In addition to the regular meditation habit, Shilyh enjoys other quick practices or mini- meditations throughout the day, especially "five-two-seven" breathing. To do this, you inhale to a count of five, retain the breath for two and exhale for a count of seven. Long, slow exhales soothe the nervous system. Shilyh finds herself claiming moments she might previously have missed, like waiting in the carpool line, to turn off the radio and practice a few moments of breathing.

In addition, Shilyh uses meditation as a resource for her whole family, like when her oldest son was going through a hard summer and was struggling to fall asleep. They did a guided meditation every night at bedtime for two months, which helped him relearn ways to relax and prepare for rest at the end of the day. Shilyh loves sharing breathing techniques and other tools with friends when they are having a hard time. "We all struggle!" Shilyh explains, "But with meditation, I feel like I've shifted out of a state where my thinking was controlling me and instead I am empowered to relate to my thoughts and internal frequency in a new way."

Dealing With Thoughts During Meditation

Meditation is an opportunity to be with yourself without feeling the need to change anything (which ironically opens the door for many things to change). There is a wealth of information about meditation in popular media and online and it can feel kind of overwhelming.

The practice itself is really quite simple. For most of us, it involves sitting in a comfortable way that allows your back to be elongated (either cross-legged or in a firm chair) and committing to placing your attention on your breath or on a mantra for a set amount of time. I recommend eight to twenty minutes. It takes approximately five minutes for the mind to settle, so if you only do a five-minute regular practice you are doing the hardest part over and over without getting as much in return.

I prefer a breath practice but sometimes I use the mantra "*maranatha*," an ancient Christian prayer word. (For more on Christian meditation visit the World Community for Christian Meditation at www.wccm.org.) Another beautiful mantra option is the Sanskrit phrase "*ham sah.*" Repeat "*ham*" (pronounced like "hum") on the inhale and "*sah*" on the exhale. You don't focus on the meaning of a mantra so much as its sound, as you silently repeat it in your head.

That's it. Simple. But not necessarily easy. Why? Well, as you sit, what happens? Your mind presents an endless series of thoughts. This is one of the saddest statements I hear as a teacher: "I tried meditation and I can't do it because I can't get my mind to stop thinking."

The goal of meditation is <u>not</u> to get your mind to stop thinking. If that is your standard of success, you will inevitably fail and drive yourself batty in the process. It doesn't even work to track your progress by measuring how many times your mind drifts away from your breath or mantra. For example, I used to think "If today, I had ten thoughts (or more likely a hundred) before the bell chimes, then tomorrow I will aim to have only four or five." Achievement-based thinking does not serve us here.

The thoughts truly don't matter. In fact, they are one of the ways your body releases stress. Interestingly, the nature of the thoughts does not necessarily track with the nature of the stress you are releasing. For example, you might be caught in an endless loop thinking about a work conflict but the stress you are releasing actually has a different source, like a fight with your partner. (More on this below when we explore Meditation Style Two: Dissolving Pernicious Thoughts.)

However, if you find yourself experiencing a strong sensation in your body during meditation, which sometimes happens, that likely *does* correspond to the part of the body where you have been holding the stress. Our tissues take advantage of the restorative time of meditation to release accumulated tension.

Three Flavors of Meditation: Choose Yours

If thoughts don't matter in meditation, what does? How kind you are to yourself and your willingness to begin again. We are building an attention muscle. And the mind is like a puppy. It will wander where it wants to go. It is in the very nature of the mind to generate thoughts. One of my favorite ways to approach this experience comes from Deepak Chopra, who says that when you notice a thought, don't get too worked up about it, simply call out, "Next!" That alone could keep us pretty busy – we think up to 50,000 thoughts a day (maybe more!). So please don't be mean to the puppy. Don't shame or smack it – honestly, it does not help. Remember the first rule of meditation and *enjoy yourself*. Treat these practices as an experiment and be willing to explore what happens.

Now, for many of my clients and meditation students, starting with silent meditation totally freaks them out and demoralizes them. Listening to your mind go crazy and feeling unable to do anything about it can indeed be very stressful, especially if your inner critic is on the prowl or your inner taskmaster insists on pointing out how very much you have left to do today. Instead, I have found that a walking practice is a powerful place to start. Moving our body while we meditate releases some of the surplus stress energy that we hold inside.

I offer three meditation styles from which to choose below. While these options work well in the order that I've outlined, feel free to start with the one that holds the most appeal for you.

Commit to a specific amount of time and try it out (8-20 minutes daily for a week per practice is a great place to start), because reading about meditation is not the same thing as *meditating*. Trust that you can get what you need. Notice how you feel not just during the practice but through the rest of your day. Meditation will reveal its benefits in every part of your life.

If you run into challenges, which is to be expected, I've included some information about common roadblocks and tips for "keeping it real," related to meditating with kids, pets and uncomfortable work garments. Make sure that you read those suggestions at the end of the chapter.

I find that guided meditations are a wonderful place to start, so I have included a powerful "Dissolve Your Stress Meditation" in the Flourish Kit, which you can access for free at www.courtneypinkerton.com/flourishkit.

If you're able to identify one specific place where you practice, it will help you make meditation a habit. For me, it's in my home studio/office on a yoga mat with a cozy lambskin over it, plus a cushion to sit on. When I travel, I have to get creative. On a recent trip to attend a book marketing training, I rolled out both hotel towels and grabbed the pillow off the bed.

The best meditation is the one that you do.

PRACTICE: Meditation Style One – Walking Meditation

To avoid the most common frustration that I hear in my meditation class and elsewhere, let's skip the sit all together for this first option, shall we? No need to wrestle with your mind. Just go for a walk and try this delightfully easy practice from Thích Nhất Hạnh, the master of mindfulness and all things good: *Oui* and *Merci*. Say "yes and thank you" to life.

How to Do It

Choose a safe place where you can walk at a slow to moderate pace, uninterrupted. You might follow a trail in a city park, wander in your yard, walk circles in an empty conference room or even pace in your office. If you are in a confined space, you only need about ten feet to walk, after which you can gently turn and walk in the opposite direction. Taking off your shoes when you are inside also feels good.

While slowly walking, inhale and internally repeat "*oui...oui...oui*"; on the exhale, say "*merci....merci.....merci.*" Match your repetitions and accompanying steps to the length of your inhale and exhale. For example, you might say "*oui...oui...oui*" (three steps) and "*merci...*

merci... merci... merci..." (four steps) if, like me, your exhale is longer than your inhale.

But wait, doesn't it have to be harder than this? Um, no. It turns out that treating this meditation project as play is so much more likely to open the space for you to grow into a new routine. If you need a metric to keep an eye on, rather than noticing how many thoughts you have, try observing how much kinder you are to yourself.

How kind are you when you miss a day of meditation or aren't able to do your practice at the appointed time? How do you treat yourself when you find you are distracted and in need of redirection to the mantra and the footstep? Might you be even kinder to yourself next time? Kindness is the secret ingredient of inner growth.

PRACTICE: Meditation Style Two – Dissolving Pernicious Thoughts

When you notice you are having a thought in meditation, it is actually a really important moment. By gently redirecting your attention back to your breath, you are rewiring your brain to be more resilient and stress-hardy. This is the part of meditation that visibly changes your brain matter on an MRI scan. It is a vital and necessary part of the practice! You can't do it wrong. In meditation, spontaneous thoughts are one way that the body releases stress; and, as we learned earlier, the content of the thought does not necessarily relate to the stress that is being discharged.

How to Do It

This is a simple breath-based meditation, with a twist. To begin, set the timer on your phone. Eight to twenty minutes is what I recommend. If sitting cross-legged is uncomfortable, you can sit in a firm chair. However, try to allow your back to elongate and your chin to be gently tucked. If you are tired and you don't want to sit up, you can lay flat in a corpse pose on a yoga mat. In general, we are looking for a sweet spot in your posture that has you feeling both relaxed and alert.

Begin by simply observing what is already happening in your body. Notice which places feel comfortable (perhaps your belly feels soft or your feet feel nice and grounded) and which parts of the body feel uncomfortable (maybe you have some tension in your neck or shoulders or a tightness in your head). Notice your breath, which is alive and moving within you without your having to do anything. Gently allow the top eyelids to rest on the bottom. There is no need to squeeze them shut.

So often, we are lost in the past or we are jumping forward towards the future. Give yourself a couple of breaths to enjoy the movement of your inhale and exhale. If you find yourself immediately distracted by lots of thoughts, it can help to bring your awareness down to your belly. You can even put your hand there and, as you breathe, tune in to the rise and fall of your belly. Conversely, if you are really sleepy or sluggish, you can bring your attention on the tip of your nose and notice the change in the temperature of your inhale and your exhale, the coolness and the warmth.

As you observe your breath, at some point there will be a thought that presents itself. This is natural and normal. There is no need to chastise or berate the puppy mind. Just bring your attention back to that point in the body where you feel your breath the strongest.

Again, a thought emerges. It could be related to your job or another dimension of your life or a question: "Is it working? I don't think it is working!" It could be a thought even as benign as, "It is really quiet in here." Remember: ***As soon as you recognize that you are having a thought, you've already become more aware!***

Now, with utter gentleness, invite your attention back to the breath, knowing that in that simple movement, you are actually rewiring your brain. If you had access to an MRI scan of your brain, over time you would be able to actually *see* the changes! Evidence shows that eight weeks of practicing a half-hour of meditation per day produces significant changes in brain matter; but it's likely that benefits occur even after shorter meditation sessions and in shorter amounts of time. So don't worry about the thoughts. Treat them as your opportunity to practice.

In fact, it can be fun to identify which thoughts emerge most often for you. When you think about it there are only so many ways we can be pulled out of the present moment. Do your thoughts tend to take you to the past, to memories? Or do your thoughts pull you forward toward tasks not yet done? Or perhaps your thoughts are more likely to be in the realm of fantasy, causing you to check out or get lost in your imagination. If it helps you let go of the thought, you can even name it. "Ok, now I'm planning things," or "That is just a fantasy." Then let it go.

Enjoy your conscious breathing for the duration of your meditation. In fact, the breath is a resource for you in *every* given moment. You can reconnect to it any time you feel lost, afraid, angry or rushed. When the timer chimes, bring your awareness up from inside yourself to the back of your face, the back of your eyes and, with a downward gaze, gently open your eyes.

Finding Freedom from Thoughts

What are some of your recurrent painful thoughts? Often, mine have to do with work: "I'll never be able to complete this book on time." "What if no one comes to my retreat?" Or the shoulds. "My husband should be paying more attention to me, even though his friend is in town." "My kids should shout less and listen more."

What if you didn't believe the thoughts that popped into your head, at least not all the time? What kind of space could that open in your daily life? For here is the really empowering bit. By building our attention muscle in meditation, we become better able to notice painful or distracting thoughts *as they emerge in our daily lives* and to find our distance and freedom from them.

PRACTICE: Meditation Style Three - Loving Kindness or *Metta* Practice

Talk of self-love always freaks me out. It sounds cheesy. I understand intellectually that it's a good thing but can't easily find a doorway into self-love as a lived practice that feels authentic and not forced.

One thing I *can* appreciate is the need to stand with myself, even when I'm struggling. Perhaps you, too, have noticed that those inner critic voices get louder when you are growing or changing? When you find yourself marching in lock step with your inner critic, this is a cue for you to slow down and offer yourself some kindness.

For this purpose, I love the *metta*, or loving kindness meditation practice, which comes to us from the Buddhist tradition. It has an awkward sound to it because we don't have an exact translation for the sentiment of *metta* into

English. "Love" doesn't quite cut it – it is too multivalent. So the term "loving kindness" was coined in an effort to describe this emotion. Think of the ways you love and care for a good friend. Now imagine you could bottle this sentiment and offer it easily to yourself. This is *metta*.

Metta meditation is a much better-known cousin of the *mudita* practice we explored in Chapter 5. Whereas *mudita* is all about cultivating joy on behalf of others successes, a *metta* practice cultivates the awareness that we all desire the same basic things: safety, happiness, health, and ease in everyday life, especially in our work/earning and family relationships. They are similar but distinct.

Historically, a *metta* meditation starts with offering a set of blessings to yourself, which you then extend out to others – first a friend or benefactor, then a "neutral" person (say, your UPS delivery person) and ultimately (if you are feeling brave), to someone who irritates you or has hurt you in the past. Finally, we extend the blessings to the whole world.

Increasingly, some meditation teachers in the West flip it and invite you first to call to mind a friend or someone you love and offer the blessings to them. Then once your heart is warmed up, you can offer the kindness to yourself. This is because many of us have such a hard time generating the feeling of loving kindness for ourselves. (Apparently, I'm not alone.)

This inability to authentically offer ourselves kindness is a serious problem and a major roadblock to being happy and present. Because if we only stand with ourselves when we think that we "did a good job" or "got it right," then our love is quite fickle. In the end, we spend a lot of time trying to earn that external approval because we can't depend on ourselves to offer it.

How to Do It

There are four traditional phrases used in a *metta* meditation: "May you be safe," "May you be happy," "May you be healthy" and "May you live with ease." (This final one refers to the things of everyday life such as earning an income and family interactions. May it go well, may it not be a struggle.) First, call to mind a friend. Imagine that you could offer the phrases to her in the way that you would offer well wishes at a birthday party. "May you have a great year!" After a few rounds of the blessings, turn to offer them to yourself. "May I be safe, happy, healthy and live with ease."

Then grow the field of loving kindness by offering it out in concentric circles. After yourself, next offer the blessings to a benefactor (someone who has been a mentor to you, or opened the way), a neutral person (someone whose name you might not even know but whom you encounter frequently, like the barista at a favorite coffee shop; I like to offer it to my mailman, who I think might be depressed). Then, if you are feeling brave, offer the loving kindness to a difficult person. You don't need to jump in the deep end here and offer it to the person who has hurt you most egregiously. It could just be someone who annoys you. If this last step proves difficult, you can also imagine yourself next to the difficult person as if you are offering the blessings to both of you at the same time.

Finally, offer your blessings to the whole world. I like to start by thinking of all of those who are meditating right now, imagining them as little lights sprinkled around the globe. Remember that some of them are offering loving kindness back to you in this very moment! Then continue to stretch your kindness to offer the four phrases to pairs of opposites, for example to those who are being born right now, to those who are dying, to those who are working and those who are sleeping, to women and to men and on and on.

As you offer these blessing out to the whole world, the *metta* or loving kindness, like the rain, also falls on you. You don't have to do all of the categories every day. Just start small and grow it.

Choose Your Commitment

Meditation reconnects you to your sense of choice and freedom in each moment: freedom to enjoy your life, freedom to be with what is here, freedom to begin again. Engage your sense of choice as you design your practice this week. Take a moment right now, a few breaths, close your eyes and feel into your body. What is the right commitment for you? Could you start with a walking meditation for 10 minutes every day? Try the sitting practice in week two and *metta* in week three; or make up your own order! You can also experiment with different times of day and locations to see what works best for you. Once you find a good fit, invest in it. That will make meditation easier and build a habit.

For bonus points, share your commitment with a friend or leave a comment on my Facebook page CourtneyPinkertonCoach. I would love to read it! You could even post that you are looking to find a meditation buddy to move through the experience together. What you share may just be the inspiration someone else needs to hear. Consider sharing it on social media (and don't forget to add the hashtag #flourishformula). Social accountability is a powerful motivator that can help you follow through.

Now that you are ready to get started, I've also included a few tips for "keeping it real," which are about meditating with kids, pets and uncomfortable work garments.

Keeping it Real: Meditating with Kids

This morning, I woke up early - evidence of the extra cortisol in my system as my book deadline approaches. I put on the kettle and move my laundry while waiting for it to warm. The kitty starts meowing incessantly, awaiting the arrival of my youngest, her favorite playmate, in the living room. And the race begins. If I don't get my clothes in the dryer and another load in the washer and make my lemon water and disappear behind my studio door before one of my kids awakes, I am so much more likely to be interrupted while meditating.

They get down on their bellies and call through the vent at the bottom of the studio door: "Mom, I want to play music on the speaker, can you disconnect your iPhone?" Or "Where is your iPad? I want to play 'Shine like a Rainbow' for my pop star teddy bear to dance to!" You can see that music (and all kinds of noise) feature prominently in their custom Flourish Formulas.

In other words, my meditation works best when my children think I'm still in bed. It really works best when *they* are still in bed or after I've dropped them off at school and the house is quiet. Though they know to respect my meditation time, they are still young and forget about a third of the time. Plus, I prefer quiet to noise when I'm sitting; though, when it is noisy, I do my best to make space for it and just meditate anyway. I have found that locking the studio door and putting in those orange foam earplugs helps.

Keeping it Real: Meditating in Tight Pants

I work from home (connecting with my coaching clients over the phone and online). This means that unless I've got a speaking or teaching gig or I am leading a retreat, I live almost exclusively in yoga pants. This is a good fit for me because I am one of those hyper-sensitive-to-tight-seams kind of people. However, most of the women I work with have more varied human interactions, requiring different wardrobes. There is nothing I love more than helping them find ways to meditate, even with a busy schedule and a less-than-ideal outfit.

So let's talk about clothes. Meditating in professional wear is simply not that comfortable. You have a couple of choices. You can meditate in the early morning in your jammies. This is a time-tested practice, sometimes called RPM, as in Rise, Pee, Meditate. You can do it upon waking or you can meditate in that hinge point before you start your work day. This is my favorite time. If you are already in your snazzy outfit – maybe even at work – skip the cross-legged moves and sit upright in a chair, both feet on the ground. Taking off your shoes can feel sneaky and delicious. I highly recommend it. A lock on your office door is also extremely helpful.

You can also try a walking meditation at lunch – somewhere green if you can get out but even a ten-foot path in your office can give you enough room. Do it before you eat (it's easier to meditate on an empty stomach than a full one). Or better yet, can you change into yoga pants for your lunch hour? This might seem excessive at first but if it helps you feel fresh, open and in a good mood for your afternoon, isn't it worth it?

Again, sneaking in the self-care is part of how we keep you resourced for the big changes that you are cooking up in our world. One final option is to wait until after work, change into something fabulous and comfy and sit before you do anything else. This is the happy hour meditation and is a powerful way to transition home and feel present for the remainder of your day.

I don't recommend meditating any later than 5:00 or 6:00 pm because it is mildly stimulating. If you are looking for an evening practice, I recommend tapping (see Chapter 7 – my favorite time is in the shower at the end of a busy day) or a gratitude list.

Keeping it Real: Meditating with Pets

Our lovely marble tabby Beatrix is a fickle meditation partner. Some days, she will politely snuggle next to my feet on the yoga mat, while gently purring. Opening my eyes to see her there enjoying the sun shining through my studio window can be a real treat. Other days she can be loud and insistently meowing. Similarly, dogs can be a beautiful reminder of how to breathe deeply and relax. But they can also require a lot of attention.

When you are just getting started, it is wonderful if you can gift yourself a pet-free environment to meditate. It is simply one less sound or pull on your attention. However, I also have had clients like Shannon, for whom meditating with her kitty in her lap is a favorite moment of the day. If you want to try to meditate with your pet, simply commit to the same basic meditation – breath or mantra – set your timer and use the sounds or snuffles of your pet as an invitation to gently redirect your attention back to your practice. If that proves too difficult, then try again in another location (or put your pet in another location) next time.

Meditation is subversive in a culture where we are expected to give, to absorb information, to produce and to respond in almost every moment of our lives. This simple act of creating a pleasing, low-distraction environment for yourself to sit for eight to twenty minutes at a time is a powerful first step in this important work of detoxing your schedule, environment and nervous system so you can orient around your own truest priorities.

Ready to get started? One final step is to tune into what you are hoping to *receive* from your practice. Maybe you want to feel more present for your family, to sleep better or to be more creative or resilient in the face of a challenge. Knowing your "why" can be powerful fuel to keep you going.

Make your commitment out of an awareness of this desire, choose one practice with which to start and *mark it on your calendar*. As the five-year host of the Summer of Meditation Challenge, I have taught over five hundred people how to step over those final roadblocks in order to create life-giving meditation practices and I know that you too can do this!

Enjoy!

9 IMMERSE YOURSELF WHEN STRESS BUILDS

This is your chapter for when the wheels come off. Step I of the Flourish process is knowing what sustains you when things don't go as planned. Your heart breaks, the deal falls through, your writing coach tells you to go back for *another* draft, you feel super stuck in your current job and can't even begin to see a way forward. You are not sure you actually like your kid. Or your partner. Or you mom.

And even worse than these external factors is the fact that you are tired of trying so hard to change things *inside*. You sit to meditate and end up feeling beat up by the racing thoughts that pound away inside your head. You try to take care of your body but it is as if the anxious thoughts take all of your energy and you barely have enough left to clean your dishes, much less head to yoga.

When all you feel like doing is shaking a fist at the sky and asking, "Why is this so freaking hard?", try one of these practices instead. Not because you should. Should isn't helpful at this stage. Ignoring the pain and pushing yourself onward (even in the realm of personal development) or trying to be somehow more Zen or relaxed in the face of your stress – neither of these choices will provide relief. Instead, immerse yourself in one of the nine centering practices described in this chapter.

Playing Depleted is Playing Small

Before we go any deeper, I want to acknowledge that if you are really struggling, the suggestions outlined below may seem like cold comfort and just marks on the page. Maybe you think they are too simple to really help you now. Isn't there some more sophisticated or subtle answer?

Yes and no. The reason you might feel disappointed reading about your invitation to commit to regular green time or to try walking a labyrinth is because of all those powerful old habits that keep you busy pushing through life.

As we discussed earlier in the book, identifying the particular rocket fuel that propels you onward is what allows you some space and freedom to relate to those inner voices in a significantly new way. As you do, emotions are going to surface. Maybe you feel unworthy, frustrated or anxious as you risk stillness. This is when we stare down the inner demon that suggests that you have value only in your *doing*, not in simply *being*. Are you allowed to be inactive? To take up space and breathe and not contribute anything in return?

Many of the women I work with have powerful inner voices here telling them to "play big," "make a difference" and "change the world." And they are so attuned to the suffering of others whose lives they want to improve that it can feel self-indulgent to rest. Even if your work is not specifically in the nonprofit or the "public good" field, my hunch is that you wouldn't be reading this book if you did not care passionately about somehow moving the needle. About contributing with a capital C in your life and doing something to lighten the load for others and to make a difference.

There is so very much change needed in the world that sometimes it seems easier to just press on than to let yourself pause and *feel* the heart break. Yet, when we are sprinting through life depleted, we are not actually giving all we have to give.

Playing depleted is playing small.

When the Wheels Come Off

A few years ago, I designed and taught an online course with a colleague. She is a bright, kind person who brought her own expertise to the table. I really enjoyed creating the course with her. The problem we had related to marketing. I had learned the hard way that collaborating with friends and colleagues could get tricky once money was involved, so this time I tried to be super clear about it. We decided we would each recruit our own participants and be compensated by their registration fees (beyond a minimum amount, which we would guarantee each other for simply co-teaching the material). We talked it through, wrote up a contract and both signed it.

"Wonderful!" I thought. "It's settled." We each proceeded to market the course to our email lists and over social media and had several participants sign up. It was a great program – full of lively dialogue – and we both learned a lot while teaching it.

The trouble came one evening after the course ended when we were wrapping up some loose ends and talking about our next steps. (I even wanted to turn the course into a book we would co-write. I was that excited about the content!) In that conversation, my colleague learned how much I had earned offering the program. (I think she previously thought I had gifted it to several of the participants as a bonus for being coaching clients.) Anyway, it was more money than she had made and she was not happy about it.

She ended up calling me later and saying that she thought I should give her half of the money I had earned. My first response was habitual: "I must have done something wrong because someone is mad at me so let me do what they want!" began running through my head on a continuous loop.

But as I got away from the conversation and really sat with it, I realized that I couldn't give away a large part of my profits and betray all the intention and energy I had put into recruiting those participants.

Money has been a great teacher for me ever since I became an entrepreneur. Like many spiritually-oriented women, I have a tendency to give it all away and downplay my own efforts. What I was beginning to learn was that such an approach does not support me, my message or the clients I am here to serve. If I give too much away, my business will not be sustainable and I won't continue doing it.

I felt squeezed between two not-fun options: I could make my colleague happy and sell out myself or honor my own truth and endure the discomfort of her judging the situation unfair and not liking me. Aaaargh! This was my nightmare or, specifically, the nightmare of my Enneagram personality (Type Three), which desperately wants to stay connected and have others think well of me. It was literally excruciating to be in this pickle. "How have I ended up here?!" I thought. "We talked it through ahead of time and we signed a contract. What do I do now?"

Ultimately, the whole thing was a super valuable lesson for me about boundaries. The conflict with my colleague was also a reminder that I can't control other people's opinions of me. It was really important for me to practice standing up for myself and not bending into the person she wanted me to be or internalizing the perspective she had on the situation.

The experience also taught me that even though I might try to keep myself safe by only partnering with "enlightened" people who share my passions around the Enneagram or other awareness tools, there is no way to prevent mishaps, misunderstandings and differences of opinion. I have to be present to myself and speak my own truth (as well as listening carefully to their concerns) to find my own way forward.

Now, if that makes it seem like there is a big, pretty bow on the conflict at this point, several years later, there kind of is. I feel so much gratitude to my colleague for the lesson, even if I wish it could have gone down another way. I most certainly did not feel anything like gratitude as I was living through it, however. In fact, the whole situation hijacked my life for a couple of weeks as I processed it. All of my regular meditation and centering tools felt like they mocked me as I replayed the argument in my mind over and over again, asking myself, "How did I end up here? What have I done wrong?"

The conflict stirred up my sense of shame – that if I was really living my life correctly, I could avoid these types of situations entirely. That was the high standard I held for myself. And those were the feelings I couldn't outrun.

After days of suffering and feeling like a loser with all those gremlin voices nipping at my heels – "Hey aren't you a *holistic life coach*? Isn't it *your job* to know how to move through challenges with ease?" – my husband suggested we take the family on a hike. It was a warm Sunday afternoon in the spring and one of the first times that the five of us could all go together. Our little one was just three or four and she scrambled like a billy goat to keep up with us as we explored a new trail.

While I was taking in the beauty around me, inside I was still hammering away unable to drop the thought parade. I was desperate for something to help. To find the doorway to walk through in my brain that would make the situation right again. On that walk, everything was not magically made better. I still had to mine the experience for the lessons to take forward, which of course took time and support. But I did catch the very first hints of relief. The trees and fresh air began to metabolize some of the extra anxiety from my body and I started to realize that the arguments in my head were getting me nowhere. The hike and nature gave me a toehold, the beginning of my ascent out of that particular abyss.

The next time you find yourself in a similar state, try one of the nine practices described below. Think of them as a menu of experiences that can help you reset when nothing else seems to be working.

PRACTICE: A Menu of Nine Centering Practices

I once heard Richard Louv give a captivating interview about his book *The Nature Principle: Human Restoration and the End of Nature-Deficit Disorder,* in which he discussed how potent nature is as a healer of our mental and physical struggles. In fact, at his suggestion, some pediatricians are now offering a "prescription" of nature time to help with a variety of illnesses. Children and families can get these prescriptions "filled" at national parks. How cool is that?

Nature features prominently in these centering practices, as do art and simple mindfulness rituals like lighting a candle to remember someone you love who is going through a hard time (that person may even be you). All of these practices are designed to gently broaden your perspective. Sometimes they are all you can do, all you can offer yourself. They are experiences that, like the hike, can open you back up when you have gotten all collapsed in on yourself or your tightly held goals.

Now, you may not be so caught up in what other people think about you but you may struggle with other challenges: trying to do it all right, trying to be in control or to play your part on the team, only to discover that you can't live up to your own standards, at least not all of the time. The next time you are in one of those spirals and can't see your way out, try one of these practices instead.

Each of them roughly tracks with the Enneagram personality of the same number and has been designed to unravel some of the constriction felt by that particular type. However, all of these practices are beautiful for anyone to use at any time. While we all have one home base of our personality type, we also experience the whole range of emotions and human struggles.

I designed and selected these practices originally for a family class and you can certainly use them with the children in your home or life. However, it turns out that many grown-ups also need invitations to use all of our senses. That is part of the power in these practices.

For instance, I was invited to teach the "Mind in a Jar" meditation at the Dallas Museum of Art as part of a community art installation. I was amazed and totally charmed by the number of people who wanted to sprinkle beans in a big jug and stir it. (See the practice described for Enneagran Type Six later in this chapter.) People of all ages and speaking all different languages came forward and were drawn in, intuitively understanding the pain that we experience when our thoughts are all stirred up and hungry for relief.

1 Experiential Gardening

Nature is deeply restorative for Type One energy because of its mental health benefits. It is a balm for relieving the inner critic. Nature is also powerful for Ones because it gives them a taste of the perfection they crave so deeply but in a way that they don't have to earn or engineer. Life is unfolding, old leaves are being composted and turned into new earth. Flowers bud and bloom. Clouds come and bring the rain. Life goes on and thrives without us having to drive the show. We have the privilege of witnessing this natural perfection where nothing at all is wasted.

Gardening is a wonderful way to touch and taste this process. Consider creating an experiential or healing garden for yourself either in pots or garden beds. Container gardening is an easy way to get started. Lemon balm, chamomile, mint, and tulsi, or holy basil, make delicious tea and are easy to grow. You can find them all as seedlings at your local garden store with the exception of holy basil, which you can find in seed packets or ask your garden store to custom order for you. You can also purchase grow-your-own herbal tea kits online.

To create your garden, simply get some pots (or grow all four in one large pot), make sure they have holes and saucers underneath to allow for drainage, put some pebbles or gravel in the bottom (again for drainage), add potting soil and *voila*! Place in a sunny spot in your house or outdoors if it is warm, and water every other day or every few days when the soil feels dry.

In addition to the mindfulness practice of caring for your plants and the quiet moment to enjoy the tea, these herbs have actual healing properties: lemon balm aids with insomnia and headaches, chamomile is soothing and calming, mint supports digestion and tulsi decreases anxiety and is antimicrobial (it filters germs out of the air). To make tea, simply snip a handful or more of herbs, rinse them, place them in a tea pot or pitcher, pour boiling water over them and let them steep for five to ten minutes. It is not an exact science; go with what tastes good to you. Then strain, add honey as desired and enjoy!

2 Heart Mandala

Women who lead with this personality type are sweet and loving but can easily over-give. Twos need to remember to recognize and honor their own desires and even more broadly to recognize that they are already included in a larger flow of giving and receiving. They need to let their own hearts be held in the same way they so generously hold others' hearts.

Creating an interactive heart mandala is an art practice that draws from a simple but ancient design. Mandala is a Sanskrit word for a shape that represents wholeness. This practice is fun to do with a friend or a child but it's equally powerful to draw a mandala yourself. Invest in some luscious thick art paper, pastels or nice markers. Make it fun to create with supplies that feel good to hold and enjoy. That is the point.

Start by drawing the tiniest heart you can at the center of a large sheet of paper. Reflect on when your own heart felt contracted, perhaps connecting to how you feel when you ignore your own needs in an effort to give and serve others.

Now, draw (or have your partner draw) another, slightly larger heart which envelops the first. Continue to take turns creating the layers or rotate the paper to draw from fresh perspectives if you are creating the mandala by yourself. Get creative with color, dots or designs. Imagine yourself enveloped in the whole: God, the Universe, Love. Feel your heart's inclusion within the big picture.

When you are done you can place the mandala somewhere you will enjoy it – you might tack it up near your office or kitchen with some Washi tape (a decorative Japanese tape, which comes in a variety of colors/patterns). You might even frame your Mandala as a reminder. (Note: You don't have to display your art at all

– this is a practice for you and displaying it would simply be as a reminder *for you*. If the pressure of displaying it changes the way you feel creating your mandala, then plan to keep it tucked away in a special portfolio or folder.

The Heart Mandala is a practice you can return to again and again. Some Twos report enjoying mandala coloring books as well. However you do it, allow this practice to help you slow down and feel included in the whole.

3 Labyrinth / Walking Meditation

Threes are focused on the external goal as well as on the perceptions of others. This type really benefits from a quiet, private practice but may find it hard to be still. Walking takes advantage of a Three's bias toward forward movement.

In particular, walking a Labyrinth challenges our cultural model of success in the West and especially in the U.S. We talk about life as a linear experience: birth, growth, accomplishment, death. In contrast, the labyrinth, a 3,500-year-old archetype, portrays life as a more complex, circular pattern.

We all need space to learn, to loop over our lessons again and again and to deepen our awareness. Walking a labyrinth can be a beautiful "moving meditation" for this busy Enneagram type, allowing them to reconnect to their inner experience and ultimately to return to the world renewed and refreshed.

Labyrinths are created out of brick, stone or other natural materials. They are found both indoors and outside. My favorite was created by monks in Kentucky who planted and tended a garden of wildflowers that delineated the ancient pattern. I walked it in my early twenties.

At that time, I faced a big decision about my future: to stay in the U.S. and work as a community organizer or to head to Nicaragua with the Peace Corps. As I considered this choice, I literally lost myself in the rows of color, heady scents and spring time sunshine. When I emerged from the labyrinth, I knew in my bones which path was mine.

You can find a labyrinth near you by using the worldwide labyrinth locater at labyrinthlocator.com.

If a labyrinth is not available you can also try Thích Nhất Hạnh's simple walking practice, *Oui* and *Merci*, described in Chapter 8. On the inhale, say, "*oui...oui...oui*" and on the exhale, "*merci...merci...merci.*" We say "yes and thank you" to life.

Remember, we aren't walking to get somewhere but to observe the sensations. The idea is to relax your mind and focus on the felt experience, trusting that clarity and a renewed relationship with yourself will emerge.

4 Nature Table / Home Altar

Women who lead with Enneagram Type Four are often very soulful but can get lost in their own emotions – to the point of thinking that they *are* their emotions. For this type, the invitation is to create a special table or altar in their home. Even if you are uncomfortable with the word "altar," simply think of it as setting a beautiful table. You are the guest. This is a space where you can relax.

The idea of a "nature table" comes to us from the Waldorf approach to education and is a way of bringing the beauty of the natural seasons indoors. (Google "Waldorf nature table" for inspiration.)

How do we make our own altar or nature table? I have found that this practice is mostly about giving yourself permission.

I was inspired by a wonderful altar-maker from Puerto Rico whom I met in Divinity School. She is a human rights lawyer and, by all accounts, a very successful professional. Someone you would read as a "head" person, not touchy-feely. But she said that, at a certain point in her career, she was working on some very troubling cases and needed somewhere to put all the emotions that flowed through her during the course of a day, rather than simply trying to numb them. She returned to her roots and began creating altars for her clients and found tremendous comfort in them. In our conversations, she encouraged me to create my own altars and I haven't stopped since then.

Use all your senses to create your altar. It can be as simple as a single flower on a table or you can incorporate more beauty: a candle, a fetching image or a cloth. Incorporate elements from nature, seasonal pods, nuts or berries you find on your walk, a beautiful leaf. Currently my altar is on the top of my bookshelf and holds my singing bowl, a large single white candle in a gold lantern and a watercolor of tomatoes that my son painted. There is no right or wrong in making an altar. It is our intentionality that makes it special and gifts us the feeling of "time outside of time" when we gaze at it.

Creating a simple home altar or nature table is very comforting for women who lead with Type Four, as it reminds us that things ebb and flow and, ultimately, pass. Similarly, emotions are quite fluid. They pass through our bodies organically / energetically in about ninety seconds if we don't try to push them down or hold onto them.

A nature table or altar helps us highlight the fluctuating nature of the seasons. Life, experiences and people are always changing and evolving and yet there is a larger rhythm and meaning to all of it, which we can't always see when caught in the storm. This practice helps us to remember our place in the whole.

5 Immersion in Nature / Music

Type Five is a head type and women who lead with this personality tend to withdraw into their minds. The medicine most needed for this type is the reminder to re-inhabit one's whole body. The key word for Type Five is *immersion*. Whether it is nature or music, this centering practice is not about trying to stop the thoughts of this busy head type so much as engaging an external resource to help ground them. If this is your type, consider a green hour – one hour outdoors every day. It turns out that simply an hour outside yields serious mental health benefits. My favorite part is that nature does the work for you! All you have to do is put yourself in it. Done!

Even more powerful than a "green hour" may be some "green and blue" time near a body of water. As humans, we just respond and relax in the face of water – the way the shoreline and the horizon mirror each other has an amazing capacity to relativize woes. If possible, visit a lake or the sea and/or swim in a nearby pool. A bathtub may provide some of this type of comfort as well.

A related and fun practice for Type Five energy (perhaps on the days you can't get to the water) is listening to music. Remember this is an immersion practice, so it is not so much about *thinking* about the music as it is about playing and even singing along and feeling the vibrations entering your entire body. Music can be a fun way to make use of time in the car to help yourself re-center.

6 Mind in a Jar Meditation

Whether or not you are a Type Six, most of us can relate to a sensation I call blender brain: thoughts and emotions swirling inside of your head without relief from the manic energy. The centering practice for Type Six is one of my favorite tools to calm your nervous system. It is called the Mind in a Jar Meditation and is great for all age groups. The best part is that you can do it with simple supplies from your pantry!

To begin, choose a large clear vase, pitcher or jar. Fill it with water and gather several different kinds of dry beans and whole grains that will sink slowly in water, like rice, popcorn kernels, red or green lentils, black or red beans, green peas or oats. (Different colors of sand work as well.)

Set the vase or jar before you and consider that the water is your mind and the different ingredients are your thoughts and feelings. Sprinkle a small handful of one grain/legume into the jar, selecting a color or texture that feels right for your current thoughts or feelings. Begin to stir slowly with a large spoon or paddle so that the water swirls around.

Consider what types of thoughts you wake up with normally. Is there a fear or anxiety that troubles you as you fall asleep? Are there any emotions that frequently disturb your peace? Add ingredients representing each thought or feeling. As you add, begin to stir faster. This is how our minds are when we are in a hurry, stressed or upset. Often toxic thoughts accumulate over the course of a day. Finally, lay down the stirrer and begin to breathe deeply while you watch the jar. What happens to our minds when we breathe slowly? *The thoughts or feelings can still be there but rest peacefully at the bottom, because we know how to calm them.*

Allowing our thoughts without identifying with them offers relief; breathing slowly and quietly is a detox for the nervous system. As is the case with all forms of meditation, there is no wrong way to do Mind in a Jar and the benefits will continue long after the meditation is over.

This is a wonderful practice to incorporate into bedtime with children as it allows them to process and digest any and all fears or troubling thoughts from the day. It is surprisingly soothing for teens and grownups too. Try it! Even if you feel silly you might do this once. Just a big glass of water and a sprinkle of rice will do the trick. Don't make it more complicated than it needs to be. In the future, you may simply want to visualize the Mind in a Jar the next time you find yourself distracted by unhelpful thoughts or feelings...and breathe. (This practice is adapted from *Planting Seeds: Practicing Mindfulness with Children* by Thích Nhất Hạnh and the Plum Village Community, 2001.)

7 Pebble Meditation

When I think about Type Seven energy, the metaphor that comes to my mind is the game kids play with balloons where they keep batting the balloon up so it doesn't touch the ground. This is the energy of Type Seven in action: perpetually wanting to keep things light and on the happier end of the emotional spectrum. Yet (as in all the types), it is an energy-expensive way to go through life. We need the full range of emotional experiences – they are our teachers and help us keep an open channel to our souls or true essence.

In general, the centering practice for Sevens needs to be grounding and connecting to the earth but in a way that doesn't feel heavy or oppressive. A busy head type with lots of extra energy, it is helpful for Sevens to engage in experiences that involve mantras and tactile elements (like holding stones) to keep the mind present and engaged. Try this simple pebble meditation as a reminder to ground that floating balloon into the fullness of your body and life.

First gather four small, lovely stones. You can carry them in a pouch or in your pocket or keep them in a special dish on your desk. When doing the practice, put all four stones on one side of you and one-by-one hold each in your hand. As you hold one, say a special word or mantra silently and connect to that particular quality within yourself. Words suggested by Thích Nhất Hạnh include "fresh," "solid," "free," and "reflecting." (This last word connects to your capacity to reflect things without distorting them, your mind like a calm, clear lake.)

You can enjoy these words as your mantras or create your own personal list. "Free" often resonates strongly with people who lead with Type Seven, but it is important to remember that you have a diverse range of qualities within you. If you create your own list try to find a similar balance. The goal is to feel grounded and resourced from within.

Enjoy a few breaths while holding each stone, imagining that you can nourish that particular quality or potential with your attention. When it feels complete to you, place that pebble on the opposite side of your body and pick up the next one. When your practice comes to a close, take a moment to notice how you feel. (This practice is adapted from *Planting Seeds: Practicing Mindfulness with Children* by Thích Nhất Hạnh and the Plum Village Community, 2001.)

8 Aromatherapy

Women with this personality type report at times feeling like a "bull in a china shop." They naturally connect to such a larger- than-life energy that it can be challenging to for them to tune into subtle sensations and to even notice their own physical and emotional limits.

Smells are a great antidote for this overpowering energy. They, by definition, exist in the present moment and are subtle. But smells also draw on one of the strengths of Type Eights, who are very embodied. Many Eights I know have a great "nose." They love cooking and tasting and eating. This centering practice incorporates that great body knowing but helps Eights *notice* when they are trying to be super human and instead tune in so that they can care well for themselves. Try it the next time you can't get your cape off.

Specifically, two aromatherapy practices I recommend: rub geranium oil on your heart or chest (I like to do this when I get out of the shower) and also use lemongrass oil as needed in order to help process your anger, either simply by inhaling the scent out of the bottle, diffusing it or using roller balls (small glass bottles with a roll-on tip filled with an essential oil and a carrier oil like olive or sweet almond) to apply it to your skin. Rubbing it directly over your liver (where Chinese medicine tells us we house our anger) is even better. You can also create one of these for a child as a "heal my heart potion" or "calming potion."

Aromatherapy is a great way to connect to our emotional lives and to feel like we can help ourselves in the heat of the moment. This practice may be more of an acquired taste for Eights, who are used to locking horns with life and blowing through situations with lots of intensity but I hope you will try it. I provide a guide to my ten favorite essential oils and how to use them in the Flourish Kit at www.courtneypinkerton.com/flourishkit.

9 Nature Mandala

Nines are sometimes called the crown of the Enneagram as they are positioned at the top of the Enneagram symbol. (See the diagram in Chapter 4.) Everyone has a little bit of all nine personalities within them but this is especially true for Type Nines. They are uniquely equipped to see situations from multiple points of view and yet sometimes forget to bring their own voices to the conversation to complete the picture.

Nines often have a wonderful soothing presence. Babies and pets may respond positively to a Nine's presence. Yet Nines can putter about in life (and even in nature) engaging in activities that don't require much from them but aid them in "checking out," a process of numbing both themselves and their desires, as well as the demands of the outside world.

Our centering practice for Type Nine is meant to stir their energy a bit to invite them to "make their mark on the world." Creating a nature mandala does this even as it takes advantage of one of the Nine's superpowers: their capacity to gather up the disparate and distinct elements of life to create a beautiful whole.

How do you create a nature mandala? As we learned earlier, the word mandala comes from the classical Indian language Sanskrit. Loosely translated to mean circle, a mandala represents wholeness and can be seen as a model for the organizational structure of life itself. There is no limit to how you can create a nature mandala. You can use flower petals from a bouquet. You may want to take a basket or a bag on a nature walk and gather various elements – leaves, pods, dried sepals, whatever strikes your fancy – and create a circular design by laying them on a tray when you return home. Special locations like beaches or favorite ponds can yield gorgeous mandalas of shells and stones.

Start by creating the inner most circle and add layers of different substances as you grow your mandala. Part of the fun is the impermanence, so remember to breathe and play. Google "nature mandala" or do the same on Pinterest for a wealth of images and inspiration.

Set Yourself Up for Easy Access

This chapter may not seem relevant for you right now if things are flowing well in your life; but I hope that you will return to it when you need additional support. I also want to encourage you to identify the centering practice that most appeals to you at this point (it may track with your Ennea type or could be a different one) and ask yourself what you could do *now* to set yourself up for success. Maybe you could go ahead and locate the labyrinth nearest you (labyrinthlocator.com) or explore some local parks. Maybe you want to order some essential oils or stop by the art store on your way home from work.

When we are struggling, it can feel like work to line up the help we need or crave. Resource yourself now and it will be that much easier to use these nine practices to reset the next time the wheels come off. Plus, it feels empowering to have these strategies ready – another set of tools you know you can access if and when you need them most. Self-care and the resiliency it develops are essential to the Flourish Formula.

10 SCHEDULE YOUR FLOURISH CALENDAR

This is the step where we bring it all together. This is your opportunity to customize a life and schedule that supports *you* rather than the other way around. To do this, we need an elegant scaffolding – a greenhouse for those tender and beautiful shoots that want to grow in your personal, creative and work lives. This is how we nurture and ultimately share your greatest contributions: The Flourish Calendar.

But before I show you exactly how to create your custom Flourish Calendar (no two women's calendars ever look the same), there is one final step we need to move through. I need you to make peace with something you may have fought for years, a practice that you may wish you could opt-out of or one in which you begrudgingly participate only when you're too exhausted to continue. What is it? Rest.

Finding Your Flow

Think back over the last three to six months.

- Do you struggle to relax on vacation?
- Do you struggle even to *take* the vacation that you are allotted? Or, to design your own regular vacations if you work for yourself?
- When you do take time off, are you able to relax or do you feel a hangover of things not yet done?
- What about weekends or more regular days of rest?
- How often do you put your phone in the drawer and gift yourself a whole day (or half-day) with no electronics?
- Do you feel that deep rest is really available to you? If not, what do you think is preventing it?

Making peace with rest is really at the heart of the Flourish process. Many of my clients don't trust it, which I understand. They struggle with this step because they have internalized a faulty formula: They feel good, alive and awake only when moving quickly through their lives. They contribute, they get many things done every day and they find satisfaction both in *what* they do and in being so productive. This can almost feel like a flow state.

But there is an imbalance embedded in this equation; an assumption that the days and weeks of generative output should continue indefinitely. Productive is the normal state they expect of themselves, so when they wake up one morning tired to the bone or fuzzy-headed and unable to think or sick or otherwise less than optimal, it feels like there is something deeply wrong. They don't recognize themselves and they push on, maybe taking a half-day off or otherwise resting just barely enough to step back into their full-speed lives. Does this sound familiar?

The truth is: We are not made to be generative all the time.

In fact, like other animals, we require regular periods of rest for optimal functioning. This is true not only in our daily and nightly routines (our circadian rhythms) but also seasonally. There are whole seasons of life (which might be a few months or even longer) in which we can be very generative. During these times, we can be super productive and lean into a new challenge or opportunity. This can feel amazing! Like fierce play.

But inevitably, there will come a counterbalancing season when we need to go receptive, to drink in and restore. This is what we often resist, largely because we aren't taught to expect it. Yet, the more attentive we are to this dynamic, the more we can capitalize on our productive seasons and allow ourselves renewal as needed.

Ultimately, deep rest is the most efficient way to get back to an inner equilibrium. Think of an infinite loop: generate, rest and repeat.

Making peace with this new formula requires a counter-instinctual move. You have to acknowledge all those neural pathways you have formed related to being busy. They aren't just yours. They are a cultural norm that you have internalized – an anxiety static passed from person to person in workplaces, homes and communities. Think of how many times you ask someone how they are and they answer, "Busy!" We pride ourselves on being busy. It is a badge of honor.

I reflected on this theme of resisting rest last summer when I had all three children at home and was working around my family's schedule. Not because we couldn't have enrolled our children in camps but because I found myself actually craving the down time with them. I wrote about this experience in a blog post at that time:

> I have spent so many years suppressing my urge to rest, I came to mistrust it. Long after I have built a life and a business centered around intuition, meditation and self-care, I am unearthing another layer of self-deceit: *I think I have to drive the show (in my life and biz) or nothing much gets done.* But lately, all I feel like doing is floating through my days with my children enjoying the home that we have created. Playing with the toys that require thick

imagination, reading the big books, picking back up with unwatched episodes of favorite shows, listening to the toll of the church bells down the street and reclining at the neighbor's house with the pool.

And more delights: Harry Potter (three of us reading this series for the first time in one house!), travel memoirs, spicebush herbal tea made from ingredients that I harvested on an edible landscape tour during our recent vacation in the Carolinas. And the butterflies that show up, sometimes in glorious pairs outside my kitchen window, bright orange and flitting between my son's mandarin tree and the zinnias I potted this spring with their bursts of red and yellow.

But can I trust myself to go over this edge? To float on these waves of doing as little as I can manage? Lazily dipping my hand in my business, wondering what it needs to keep rowing forward and doing only that, one stroke a day. Sometimes, only a stroke a week.

And my home – one extra household task a day to keep the tidy equilibrium is all I can muster on top of the daily dishes and meals. Putting away two loads of laundry is an accomplishment. Will I ever return from the land of hazy rest? Or will

I forever drift down this river and, when I emerge, be disoriented, wondering what happened to my life and my work?

Yet, here is the strange thing: during this month of doing nothing and fasting from social media, I acquired several new coaching clients, was invited to teach a weekend retreat in the spring and received a request to design a wellness theme for parents and teachers at a local school. I've also been able to capture a handful of writing snippets as they emerge. And I am enjoying appointments with current coaching clients while my husband or babysitter care for the children, showing up grateful for the quiet and the chance to be with just one person and to listen deeply, a respite from the multi-tasking and continuous demands that populate my mama life.

In short, something is moving, but it has such a different quality than my own ego-hewn sense of how work should feel. It feels light. Driven by a fuel far distinct from my narrow-focused sense of the work equation: Time at my computer screen = productivity.

As I sat yesterday and listened to my friend talk about her recent visit to a shaman (how do I find a shaman?!) I felt the world quivering at my feet, the grass moving and bending, the leaves dancing, the vibration of life surrounding me, this green nation converting sunlight into its own sustenance. What if our relationship to our own life and livelihood could feel like that? As intuitive? As self-nourishing?

I am coming to trust the river of rest and to know that there is an end to how long I will even want to float in this place. At some point, it feels good to get out of the water, your fingers all wrinkly, and enjoy the rub of a towel warmed on the beach. And the hunger in your belly invites you to work again, to start the fire.

This is what I am coming to learn: My appetite for silly movies will fade, depositing me grateful and open-hearted in the real-life web of human and nonhuman relationships where I make my home. My impulse to lay and read another travel memoir will transition to dreaming and research about an upcoming trip to the mountains of Mexico to celebrate a big birthday. I will eventually want to wash my hair and to cook a hot meal of fresh beet greens and basil and an omelet of goat cheese from the farmer's market, all a-drizzle with the Palestinian olive oil that we received as a gift. And to reconnect to more coaching, teaching and writing.

In short, rest deposits me back into my life, now more awake to its subtleties. More grateful. I won't get lost there, I can trust it. And so can you.

The Sensual Pause

Please know that all those busy impulses will continue to fire and feel familiar and to push you forward at an unsustainable pace. Reading one book will not stop them. And all the steps we have explored so far – the Enneagram, mind-body practices like tapping and meditation, etc. – will fall to the side of your life ineffective without one secret intervention, what I call the sensual pause.

What do I mean by sensual? I mean being in and alert to your body as well as using all of your senses. (I am indebted to coach Tara Marino for this definition of sensual.) You can start by taking three sensual breaths the next time you feel the inner pressure cooker imploring you to move on to the next task. Even one breath can be enough. To get very specific, I'd like to invite you to practice a breathing pattern called five-two-seven breathing. Breathe in for a count of five, hold for two and release for a count of seven. Long, slow exhales are calming to our nervous system. Try one five-two-seven breath right now. Feel free to continue if it feels good.

And then, I want you to simply notice the familiar get-more-done energy. Make room for it in your experience (meaning don't make yourself bad or wrong for this habit) but see if you can check in with it from your more spacious perspective. This is the sensual pause. Simply gift yourself a moment in order to *consciously* choose.

For me, many of these tensions arise between my children, whom I love, and my work, which I also love. This morning, I was up early writing, which is my best time to write. I don't normally work on the weekend but the ideas were flowing, the sun had risen and my hot lemon water was next to me on the desk. After about an hour of this, my kindergartener Rosetta pops into the office, dressed and ready for a play date. She needed my attention to help with breakfast and get her hair in a ponytail and otherwise start her day.

Feeling some regret about leaving my writing (what if the muse doesn't come back?), I stepped into the kitchen hoping I could help her and return quickly. After I got her breakfast she asked, "Do you want to play a game?" "Errr," I thought, feeling the pull back to my desk. One sensual breath later, I remembered my deeper intention to be more present to her. Rosetta has a different personality than her older siblings and thrives with more social contact. (I think she might be our only extrovert.)

I ended up having fun playing a few rounds of twenty questions with her while I unloaded and reloaded the dishwasher (hey, that urge to be productive doesn't go away...) and also sat down and enjoyed my breakfast, tea and some reading from the Desert Mothers (a group of fierce spiritual teachers from the 4th century). Once Rosetta was picked up for her play date an hour later, I was able to drop back into my writing.

Now in a different moment, I might make the opposite choice. Sometimes my children or family need to understand that my work is important too, whether I'm organizing the school garden, writing, coaching or preparing for a retreat. But the point is that with the sensual pause, I get to *choose* what feels like my most inspired next step, rather than run on autopilot and let the never-ending to-do list rule my life.

The sensual pause is almost always about being generous. In some cases, it is about being more generous with yourself and setting a boundary around work or other priorities that you hold dear. In other cases, it is about being generous with another and relaxing how you thought your day would go to reconnect to your deeper or more loving priorities. Like this morning, when I suggested that my husband go to the coffee shop for some unplanned alone time when I realized that our house renovations had overloaded his circuits. Pausing is about peeling those little fingers of control off of your life, dropping the scarcity mindset and relaxing the idea that there isn't enough time for you to live into the size and scope of your ambitions.

You may need more than a few breaths to feel into your truest priorities. In that case, check in with your Flourish Calendar, go outside for five minutes, do some secret yoga in your office or otherwise reconnect to your desire to live a spacious and fulfilled life, on your own terms. Then make your choice and resume.

PRACTICE: Schedule Your Flourish Calendar

Now, what if you are genuinely so busy that to stay afloat in the sea of all of your commitments, you must continuously be going full out? What if there is realistically not room to rest or play as you desire? Then you may need more than a sensual pause to reset. In fact, your life may be inviting you into more significant shifts. Finding your optimal life rhythm depends not only on how you hold your days but on an elegant edit of what fills them. The Flourish Calendar is a huge ally in this process.

Many of my coaching clients are tired. As we discussed in previous chapters, sometimes an early bedtime or a nap is the next best step towards discerning the life that wants to live out of you. Other times, that fatigue indicates a need for more targeted activity, honoring *your* true priorities.

This could mean time to exercise or move your body in a way that you truly enjoy (like taking a big walk by the lake); or it could mean investing in and sharing your genuine passions. For example, if photography is a growing interest for you, consider selecting your favorite images from a backlog of digital photos to print and share with others.

If you are physically tired or fatigued by a life that no longer fits you, the Flourish Calendar can help. Read on to learn how to craft your own.

Do the Groundwork

First, answer the following questions in your journal or on a piece of paper:

- How do you imagine your life will *feel* when you have more whitespace in your schedule?
- How do you prioritize your time currently (by category of activity)?
- Do you have space to be intentional or do you feel mostly reactive?
- What priorities do you have that currently don't have a regular home in your calendar? This could be alone time, time to write, quality time with a

partner, time to explore a hobby or time to make significant progress on big work or creative projects, rather than just putting out fires.

Now it is time to create a framework wherein you give every day in your week a "job" or a role on your calendar. These roles will be unique to you and your work and your home commitments and of course, not every day will follow this pattern perfectly. But it is very helpful to have a basic recipe for structuring your time, especially those tasks that are a perennial part of your life.

For instance, Mondays are my day to catch my breath and nurture my business; so I have no client work that day, but instead focus on financial management, invoicing, filing and web and social media updates. On Tuesdays and Wednesdays, I have my one-on-one coaching sessions with clients. Thursday is for group coaching and teaching preparation. (I teach usually a few times a month on an evening or Saturday. If I work on a weekend, I try to take a day off that next week.) Friday is a flex day – it always includes my favorite yoga class and writing and sometimes catching up on other things so I can wrap up my workweek with a sense of completion. Saturday and Sunday are family/free days and once a month is a school garden workday.

How might you best "batch" or aggregate the different types of work/activities in your week? Although, in the previous example I offer groupings perhaps more relevant for service-based entrepreneurs, you can design categories that make sense for you whether your work is primarily at home or at a more traditional job.

For example, if you work within an organization, you may have several standing meetings on a weekly basis and chunks of your time may be dedicated to team processes. Nevertheless, you likely also have some discretionary time in which to focus on your own work priorities. Identify these work categories and consider how you can group those activities in ways that allow you to uni-task more and multi-task less.

Step by Step Process: Create Your Flourish Calendar

Step 1: Gather Your Supplies

Buy a paper calendar (remember those?) or print your Flourish Calendar template from the Flourish Kit at www.courtneypinkerton.com/flourishkit.

Gather your supplies: markers, pencil or pen and a cup of tea or favorite beverage. Use in conjunction with your Google Calendar, iPhone Calendar or other primary calendars you use to keep track of your life. I like to have my Google Calendar open on my iPad and sit at the kitchen table. Find what feels good.

Step 2: Set the Timer

Set the timer on your phone for twenty minutes. I find that putting myself in a "time box" helps me stay focused. This is your time to uni-task. Shut down the computer and focus on the big picture. And remember, this calendar is the bird's eye view that helps you prioritize your soul goals and remember the freedom you have to create them. It may also take you longer the first time you create a Flourish Calendar. If it does, just reset your timer for another twenty minutes until you complete it.

Step 3: Color-Code Your Days

Write the specific dates for this month on your calendar. The template is blank so that you can reuse it. Remember the basic categories for prioritizing your time that you identified in the questions in the previous section and search for the overall pattern. For example, every week I have days when I work *on* my business (strategy, bookkeeping, marketing, preparing for group programs or speaking opportunities) and days when I work *in* my business (coaching clients, teaching retreats). I also have a day to write and free days or what I like to call

Flourish Days. (I am indebted to coach Sage Lavine for inspiration related to calendaring.)

Those of you who have your own businesses may want to distinguish similarly between working *in* your business (clients) and *on* your business (strategy). If you work in a larger organization or have a traditional job, consider the various kinds of work you do on a regular basis. As we discussed earlier, you may have less control to completely dictate your calendar at work but I'll bet that you have some flexibility to aggregate certain tasks. Similarly, if your work is centered on caring for your family, your schedule may feel more open-ended; but that can present its own challenges. It helps to dedicate blocks of time for your own priorities.

Also consider those creative and other aspects of your life that may currently be under-expressed. Perhaps you want to invest in your own writing or to carve out time for a regular massage or other body care.

You may not be designating whole days but can also specify half-days or special evenings, i.e. Thursdays are my night to go for bike rides with my family. The goal is to create intentional time to listen, explore, and *develop your own priorities*. Color-coding is super helpful here. Create a simple key for the different kinds of days that fill your life and highlight the calendar accordingly.

For example, on my calendar:

Blue = Flourish Days (more on this in a moment)

Green = working *in* my biz: meeting with clients, group coaching, teaching, retreats

Orange = working *on* my biz: strategy, back office work, marketing and preparing for teaching, etc.

Step 4: Remember to Include Activities You Love

Consider how often your calendar is filled only with obligations and to-dos, appointments and requirements on your time. It is so important in our culture of workaholism, in which we never get to truly feel "off," to also schedule activities, outings and hobbies that you love. For instance, on my weekends and other free time I write down yoga, volunteering, date nights, travel, hikes and nature outings. I call those free days Flourish Days because they remind me to stretch back out into the fullness of who I am. And it feels very good to see them taking up space on my calendar.

It is vital to choose a word here that resonates for you. Maybe they are not your Flourish Days but your "Free Days," your "Awaken Days" or your "Renew Days." Choose a word that feels good, one that gives you that soul ping of recognition. "Yes, this is what I desire, this is the life I crave."

An important caveat: It may be that your weekends or other traditional rest days actually feel like *more* work, especially if you have young children at home or other responsibilities during that time. If that's the case, we may need to get creative about when and how you schedule time for your own deepest priorities.

In my family, my husband and I take turns. Saturday mornings are my times to write or read or take a bath or do whatever brings the most relief and joy into my life that week. So sometimes, it is doing the thing that I most need to do. For example, this week I went shopping for professional clothes for an upcoming speaking engagement. I don't actually love shopping but taking that time for myself and enjoying the results feels really good. But most Saturday mornings, I opt for regenerative time away from the computer and phone with some favorite reading or lounging while my husband takes the children out for breakfast and fun so I can have a quiet home. In turn, he enjoys a couple of evenings a week after dinner for Karate and writing.

Step 5: Add Your Self-Care and Holistic Body Practices

Make sure to weave your own holistic or body care practices into your regular schedule. You don't have to wait for a collapse; build them in along the way. For me, these are regular acupuncture and chiropractic sessions. (Return to Chapter 7: Understand the Language of Your Body for more ideas on how to be the CEO of your own wellbeing.) Far from being indulgent add-ons, regular maintenance appointments save you time in the long run as they keep your immunity and energy levels functioning optimally.

Step 6: *Enjoy* the Space Between the Notes of Your Life

Creativity thrives within a constraint. It shows up when we do and when it has a lovely container. If we want to be able to discern our most potent contributions, we need space between the notes of our lives and room in our schedules to breathe. This will require elegant boundary setting. Remember, this is your one wild and precious life and you cannot be all things to all people. (We will talk more about this in Chapter 11 on Obstacles.)

For now, brew some tea, set the timer on your phone for twenty minutes, grab your calendar and some markers and create your Flourish Calendar for the current or next month (if this month is already too full of obligations). I actually like to do two months at a time or at least include the first week of the next month when I do my calendar so that I have some space to coast before I have to make another one.

If your work and responsibilities allow some flexibility in scheduling, try to bundle your work and create a Flourish Week every month. This is graduate level Flourish calendaring, so you may have to build up to it. I have been experimenting with this practice for the last year and I must say it feels amazing. Sometimes my Flourish Week is for an actual family vacation, holiday, or travel. Other times it just allows me time to attend to deeper priorities. Like having friends visit without feeling squeezed, or like this month, when I am using my Flourish Week to finalize the edits on this manuscript.

If that feels overwhelming or is not realistic, don't worry about it for now. Simply remember to breathe and have fun! Tack your calendar up somewhere you will see it regularly and, for bonus points, snap a picture and share it on my Facebook page CourtneyPinkertonCoach.

Conclusion

What one step could you take this week to bring your rest and creative output closer to an equilibrium? Do you need more sleep to enjoy your days? Try going to bed fifteen minutes earlier and see how you feel. Or do you need to find some support to bring your dreams and desires to life? Creating your Flourish Calendar is a good first step.

Wherever you are in the cycle of rest or sharing your creative or professional gifts, remember that this way of managing our lives is an iterative process, not a one-time fix.

In fact, this step is a common challenge point as women move through the Flourish process. If you would like to explore the options for additional support, I invite you to visit my website: www.courtneypinkerton.com.

I hope this chapter helps you to navigate your days – some floating, others paddling through the rapids – and at the end of each, to look around and recognize that at rest or at work, you are still very much at home.

11 OBSTACLES

It's time to talk about the four main obstacles that will keep you from both the impact and enjoyment of life you desire (if you let them). The Flourish process is not a sequence written in stone but rather a way of life, so when you hit these obstacles, which come up at some time or another for all of us, take them as an invitation to re-engage, recalibrate and let yourself start again.

Obstacle 1: I Don't Have Enough Time

This is what it really comes down to isn't it? This phrase is such a powerful gremlin for so many women. If you repeat it to yourself again and again it becomes entrenched and you don't even realize it's a painful or limiting thought. It just seems so.... true.

Given the power of this phrase, I would certainly expect this obstacle to pop up again and again. As we discussed earlier in the work chapter, reading one book is not going to completely eradicate it and you don't have to figure out how to make all of the shifts you are interested in making overnight. It just doesn't work like that. We heal a layer or wake up to an aspect of life where we have been sleepwalking and from this new vantage point we can see our way forward.

So please don't let the fact that you "don't have enough time" keep you from taking some small, targeted action. In fact, I love the phrase, "start before you are ready." It's brave to risk spending some of your precious time and energy on this book, which is largely about inner exploration. At first it can feel like a waste of time when there are flashing lights and important projects and social media all calling relentlessly for your attention.

A thousand protests might come to mind at the idea of taking time to integrate the practices in this book into your daily life. Nevertheless, I am inviting you to really hold yourself accountable to the deeper priorities that motivated you to pick up the book in the first place and to follow through. That will help you build a relationship of trust with yourself. It will fuel your rapid movement through these eight steps and any other challenges that pop up and threaten to derail your slow-down-and-change-the-world mojo.

Showing up for yourself in this way will also guide you in editing out the nonessentials so you can gain clarity regarding bigger changes that may be rumbling. Things like a new job or career, moving to another city or writing the book you feel beckoning within.

If you are feeling squeezed for time remember what we talked about in Chapter 3 and honor how you normally like to make changes in your life.

For example, you may be someone who prefers to break a large project into small pieces and tackle a bit of it every day. If so, then weaving dedicated Flourish time into your regular daily or weekly routine will likely work best. You could do these practices on your lunch break – bonus points if you can get out of the office and head to a nearby park or green space. You could move through them at the kitchen table first thing in the morning or on the weekend.

Or you may want to implement several changes at once by taking yourself on a solo retreat to work through the material in this book and create a new plan.

These are not either/or options. In fact, the most delicious way to integrate these practices into your regular life is to do both. But we don't want you climbing uphill, especially when facing the "not enough time" concern, so I invite you to honor your preferences and make yourself a date or several dates to be with your most spacious self and these Flourish exercises.

Obstacle 2: Guilt, Shame, and Anxiety

The eight steps of the Flourish process are wonderful tools but they can't compete against unexamined and entrenched emotions. In fact, some of the tools we explored in the previous chapters (e.g. meditation, nature and sleep) may already be on your list of things to try but they may linger neglected at the *bottom* of the list, where they just make you feel guilty. There is such a difference between *knowing* that you should be doing something and trying it in real life.

What opens that door and allows you to actually live into the Flourish steps? Calling out for yourself (with total kindness) those emotions that keep you stuck in your overachieving pattern. For most women they are guilt, shame, anxiety or some lovely cocktail of all three.

Are we simply stuck if the intensity of these emotions overrides the potential of the Flourish tools? No. These emotions are so much more powerful when they are unexamined, so let's just examine them. This brings them into the light of your awareness, where you can *feel* them (remember, it only takes ninety seconds to let an emotion move energetically through your body).

Once you let yourself feel them as they emerge – that is, if you don't hang on to them or push them away – these feelings dissipate. This frees up an enormous amount of energy in your life! Energy you can direct towards conscious living. Think of this as the companion project to everything that we have explored in this book, especially those gremlins or painful thoughts. These are just the emotional equivalents.

Let's be really clear: Guilt, shame and anxiety are certainly not bad and please don't make yourself "less than" or wrong for feeling them, as it only drives them in deeper. It is just that they don't have the juice to get us where we want to go. You know what does? Love. Fierce, shining love. The way to move through guilt or other painful emotions that keep you locked in proving, exceeding and pushing is to find a way to authentically love yourself. There is nothing inside you that will be powerful enough to fuel these changes unless you find some way to love yourself for wanting them.

How to love yourself is, in some ways, a whole other book (and indeed there are a gazillion on that very subject). But at the same time, it could be as simple as living into these eight steps from a place of genuine kindness and concern for yourself. That *is* a form of love. And it can be authentic. We only get so many trips around the sun and that deeper, wiser part of you knows that you can either really commit to learning these lessons now or you can press on at an unsustainable pace until something else stops you and forces you to learn them – maybe you get really sick or a personal or professional tragedy opens your heart in a new way.

It is totally your choice to make; but why not go ahead and learn them now? If you are really serious about wanting to make your greatest contributions in this life, you may need the extra years of living at a conscious and sustainable pace to really mine and share them. Later may simply be too late, not only for you to adjust your pace but also for you to have the energy to create to your fullest.

Obstacle 3: The Need for Other People's Approval

The third obstacle has to do with your relationships and social connections. Taking the time to cultivate the inner life is a countercultural move when most of us are addicted to speed. You are in the master class of life and time management here and most women honestly don't do this or know how to do it. If you were to put down the book, look around and start asking your friends or colleagues for their opinions about your life, those conversations would likely muddle your process.

I saw this phenomenon when I used to support women as a doula. Pregnant women would ask other mothers about their birth stories and, in looking for answers or inspiration, would end up the undeserving recipients of undigested pain and messy advice born out other women's challenging experiences. Much of this only served to demoralize or frighten the pregnant mom.

Many, many women talk themselves into boxes. They are caught in webs of obligations on their time which no longer fit or serve them but from which they don't know how to extricate themselves gracefully. There is a lot of pain in our culture around this tender subject of work/life balance, so don't go opening that conversation with everyone unless you are ready to absorb some of their confusion.

Now if there is a woman in your life who genuinely (not on the surface but all the way through) seems to be making a serious contribution and enjoying the pants off her personal life, feel free to talk to her about it. In my experience, such women are rare but extremely generous. While they are happy to share some of what they have learned – and it can be truly inspiring – they also know that they don't have the answers for *your* Flourish Formula.

You may also find that the most important people in your life – your husband, partner, parents, friends, even children – struggle with the changes that you are making. They may say they don't recognize this "new you" or express discouragement about directions you want to explore. While uncomfortable, this experience is to be expected. In fact, it is so common it has a name: "The change-back attack."

There are many reasons why this happens. Perhaps your shifts are threatening to your family and friends in some way – or remind them of unrealized desires they harbor within. You may never know what it stirs within them and, truthfully, you don't need to. Remember that all awareness work begins *within*, so if you are inspired to initiate some changes in your life after reading this book, don't look to have those impulses validated by those around you. Just keep all that juice and truth within yourself and *do the work*. This may well open up all kinds of interesting conversations down the road as people are drawn to you like honeybees watching you bloom and wondering what has shifted for you. If that starts to happen, fabulous! It is more fruit borne of this journey. But for now, know that we start inside with what pings true and is inviting for you.

There is one exception to this caution on inviting others into your process and that is the accountability partner. Do you have a friend or other connection with similar priorities, who might like to walk with you through this process? If so, having a buddy can be an extremely powerful way to proceed. You can retreat together and/or check in every other week or monthly, in person or on the phone.

If you are interested in taking these steps within a supportive coaching relationship, I hope you will reach out to me at www.courtneypinkerton.com to schedule a Flourish Design Call and explore your options.

Truthfully, weaning off of external validation can be really challenging, so do consider what would help you the most right now and create it for yourself. Working within a supportive relationship can help you stay true to yourself and offer much-needed encouragement throughout the process.

Obstacle 4: Your Inner Perfectionist

Finally, remember that all of those old overachiever habits are now going to circle around this new Flourish framework. But you are on to them. You don't have to let them derail your growth journey. Instead, remember that one of the key obstacles for a go-getter is to try to adhere to this framework (or any framework) "perfectly."

This happened to me when I first learned the Enneagram. I wanted to be the healthiest Type Three possible. Doing the Enneagram became my job (no Type Three habits there, wink!); but making the Flourish tools and techniques into another box to check seriously diminishes their transformational power. Instead of approaching this process from a place of pushing, striving and (inevitably) judging yourself for coming up short, I want to invite you to hold it in a more dynamic and flexible way.

It is like the moment in meditation when you realize that a certain thought has carried you away. That is where the magic happens, when you rewire your brain by bringing your attention back to the present. Likewise, when you realize you are holding these steps with a death grip, see if you can laugh at yourself a little, take a deep breath, offer yourself compassion and begin again with a lighter touch. Remember the true custom Flourish Formula is not in the book you hold in your hands but is born out of your own intuition, heart and deepest essence.

In short, expect to fall down on your Flourishing journey. These are some of the major stumbling blocks you may encounter but there are likely to be a few unexpected ones as well. Know that you don't have to do it perfectly. Instead, choose to take a sensual breath, open yourself to the beauty around you and begin.

12 YOUR FLOURISH FORMULA

"The plain fact is that the planet does not need more successful people. But it does desperately need more peacemakers, healers, restorers, storytellers and lovers of every kind. It needs people who live well in their places. It needs people of moral courage willing to join the fight to make the world habitable and humane. And these qualities have little to do with success as we have defined it."

— Dalai Lama

I have a secret agenda. In addition to helping you slow down, I want you to be a well-resourced revolutionary. I'm not sure if women's leadership voices have ever been more needed, at every level. It's time for women to stop operating from states of depletion and exhaustion and to start modeling the wholeness we want to create in our communities. This book is your how-to guide. I don't think you would be here reading it if your voice and inspiration were not vital to the shared story we are writing on this planet.

It's hard to leave you here, knowing that there are so many questions left to be answered and so many details of your Flourish Formula yet to be discovered.

I hope that each chapter has equipped you with a fresh resource to try on, to play with and to integrate in your journey of slowing down, which is really a journey of becoming more alert and mindful. At times, we may forget what we have learned and numb out and race through life toward the finish line again; but it gets easier and easier to shake ourselves out of that trance and recommit to full-on presence to the beauty (including the heartaches) of life. This is where the magic happens, where your change-the-world gifts can be most fully mined and expressed, starting with transforming your own life from the inside out.

The example that you set can be a step towards changing the world. Imagine the children you know, either your own or others, looking to you and knowing that they don't have to sacrifice themselves – their wellbeing and happiness – to make a difference. What if they came to understand by watching *you* that they could really invest in their gifts *and* find their quality of life blossoming as well? What kind of world could that create?

Even if the whole world is not on board with our Flourish project, we can create subversive slow-living pockets and communities that shine, revealing the depth of relationships, meaning and beauty that come from hearing the siren's call of "Faster!" and risking another path.

So much of what we see depends on the speed at which we are traveling. It turns out, for example, that we miss many of the interactions of other species in our world simply because our eyes and ears are not attuned to their frequencies. The hummingbird doesn't just hover. It dances, flips and dips through the air, swooping in and out of flowers, trailing nectar and appearing drunk with life. Without time-lapse technology, all of this movement is simply lost on us; our eyes cannot take it in.

Our eight Flourish steps are designed to retrain your mind, heart and your entire body's neural pathways from the speed addiction of our culture and tune them to an alternate frequency. **Finding the way out of the box you are in** with the Enneagram is the first and pivotal step. **Learning how to see your work as a love affair with life** rather than a tortuous web of comparing and despairing is the second step. Realizing that those inner critical voices actually get louder when we are growing and learning how to **overcome the gremlins** is our next step. It is followed by coming to speak and **understand the language of your body**. This allows you to better digest the natural stresses in your life (which we can never completely avoid) and keep them at a healthy level. This will help you avoid body breakdowns exacerbated by chronic stress and simply feel good in your life.

Next, we explore several meditation techniques that equip you to **reset when the pressure builds** (and detox your nervous system on a regular basis). We continue with a menu of centering practices in which you can **immerse yourself** the next time you feel caught in the old anxieties and when nothing else is working. Finally, we have a step-by-step exploration of how to **schedule your own custom Flourish Calendar** so you can bring all of these changes in practice and awareness into your daily life.

What about the "H" in Flourish?

The H in the process is simply a reminder to **hold it lightly**. Any coaching or personal growth book can end up feeling static or formulaic. The truth is that there is creative tension embedded in this prescription: Your Flourish Formula will require both flexibility and follow-through. Play and experiment with the practices and make the process your own; but if you don't really commit to it, your blind spots may keep you from the outcomes you desire.

For me, hold it lightly means don't use these recommendations to beat yourself up or otherwise judge yourself harshly. As I've shared before, this all-or-nothing attitude to change actually gets in our way. Hold it lightly but do hold onto the Flourish process. Make this book your talisman or your good luck charm. Keep it somewhere special and come back to it as needed for encouragement or to deepen in a particular section.

Bringing it All Together: Meredith's Story

Meredith is a busy media consultant and entrepreneur. She lives in Boston with her husband, who works long hours in the engineering field. When we spoke a few weeks ago, Meredith felt like the wheels were coming off her life. She was not feeling as connected to her husband as she would have liked, there was some family drama brewing related to her brother's new wife (she always seemed to get roped into it) and she was missing her old neighborhood after a recent move.

Her friends were troubled by her bleak outlook and said that they didn't recognize her. They were used to her being more bubbly and upbeat but the outcome of the recent election had left her in a serious citizen depression. Meredith felt lost and frustrated as the practices that usually helped her seemed to not be working. She was barely doing yoga (even though she is a yoga teacher!) and she was coming to resent her meditation practice as she found herself sitting there steaming and looking for a way to fix what seemed so wrong in our country and in her personal life.

During her coaching session, we explored some very simple strategies for Meredith to slow down and be with these uncomfortable sensations without needing to fix or otherwise do anything about them. Remember how when we try to change ourselves in a harsh way we often end up reinforcing our old habits? And conversely, when we find a way to be with who we are, even if we don't like it, things often begin to shift? That is exactly what happened in Meredith's life.

Two weeks later, when we connected next, she was like a new person. She had spent a wonderful weekend unplugged with her husband at a nearby cabin, enjoying skiing and real connections with him and another couple. She enjoying a meaningful phone call and lunch date with two good friends who reached out to her. And Meredith discovered what she had been looking for (without knowing exactly what that was) in a neighborhood group through which she met several local activists. They encouraged and invited her into a whole web of opportunities to express her political values in ways that felt concrete and productive.

Of course, these opportunities didn't come out of nowhere; but they almost felt like they did. In slowing down, Meredith had gotten really clear about the things that were most important to her in her life (which she hadn't been prioritizing) and the opportunities to reengage them appeared. She is now enjoying her meditation practice again and her whole mood and outlook have shifted.

I have seen this experience play out in my own life and in the lives of clients again and again. Slowing down isn't itself the magic elixir (although, in a way, it is because it gives your nervous system a chance to catch up and reset); but when we are living out of our fight or flight response or that whack-a-mole reactive energy, we don't even know what we are hungry for. Slowing down gives us space in our minds and hearts to get really clear about what is important to us and this clarity is powerful.

Slowing down is not something you do one time. It is a practice you get to engage in again and again. Meredith was able to experience dramatic results in a short time frame largely because of the deep foundation of awareness practices she had put into place over several months of working together. That is what I hope this book offers you as you move through the eight steps. It doesn't mean that you'll never veer off the overachiever recovery path again; but when you do, you will know your way back home.

I want to leave you with one of my favorite metaphors. I love traveling in Latin America and am especially charmed by painted adobe homes. There is something so beautiful about the contrast between the deep history, humility and soft, weathered edges of the structures and the explosive, luscious colors they are often painted: bougainvillea fuchsia, lemon yellow, bright turquoise.

These houses are a reminder that each of our lives is but a thin layer in the dense, centuries-old accumulation of human experience. At the same time, they encourage us to make our mark *today* and to share whatever beauty we possess. To make a decision and to go for it. One day we will be too old and someone else will get to choose the color. But today, it's our turn to paint the house.

I hope that the Flourish Formula helps you design a life that delights you and inspires others. I hope that integrating the eight steps and creating a unique framework for your life and schedule allows you to be deeply resourced, intentional and laser clear about your priorities. That is my dream for you and I believe that you can do it. I also believe that engaging the Flourish process can change your life, the lives of the people you love and, ultimately, enhance the beauty and the impact that you make in our world.

PRACTICES

FIGURES

DESCRIPTION	Page
The Enneagram	50
Enneagram Triads	59
Stress and Security Types	71
Tapping Points	146

FURTHER READING

BodyWise: Discovering Your Body's Intelligence for Lifelong Health and Healing by Rachel Carlton Abrams, MD

Deep Living: Transforming Your Relationship to Everything that Matters Through the Enneagram by Roxanne Howe-Murphy

The Desire Map by Danielle Laporte

The Essential Enneagram by David Daniels

Everyday Happiness: EFT Tapping for Self-Transformation that Really Works by Claire P. Hayes

Finding Your Own North Star by Martha Beck

Finding Your Way in a Wild New World by Martha Beck

Hardwiring Happiness by Rick Hanson

The Nature Principle: Human Restoration and the End of Nature-Deficit Disorder by Richard Louv

Real Happiness at Work by Sharon Salzberg

Soul Centered: Transform Your Life in 8 Weeks with Meditation by Sarah McLean

GRATITUDE

First and foremost, I am grateful to Spirit for being my teacher.

Also, this book owes so much to my children Coleman, Perl and Rosetta. When I was lost in my overachieving ways, they helped wake me up to my desire for a more spacious life. My ambition didn't go away but they invited me to find a new pace and container for my work and have taught me how to go on a vacation and really leave it all behind. For this and their continual invitations to play, to laugh, to dance and to think about life from a different vantage point, I am so grateful.

To my husband Richard Amory: In that moment on a rooftop in San Miguel de Allende on my 40th birthday when I said I wanted to write a book this year and you said, "I think you will do it", some part of me deep inside sat up and took notice. You, my darling, are not effusive and sunshiny, which makes your encouragement all the more powerful. For this dream and many others, you help me discern the right timing.

I am not sure either of us had any idea where this creative project would lead in our personal lives. But somehow the writing of this book quickened within me a long-term dream to relocate to Nicaragua and introduce it to our children. We made the decision together and within three months had liquified our household and sold our home. And once in Nicaragua, your contribution to this book increased from the supportive wings to a central role as editor.

I have been touched, again and again, to watch the way that you engage these ideas with care and help each component of the book to shine, as well as to integrate it into the arc of the whole. I feel like you have treated this book the way that you treat me, both loving it as it is and also seeing the deeper truth which you help, simply with your loving attention, to bring out. I am so glad that I get to live my life with you. *Te amo.*

For Lynn, who held my gaze that day on my driveway eight years ago when I told you "I feel like I'm missing it." I thought at the time I meant missing tender moments with my children because of the intensity of my work. But what I was really talking about was a feeling of missing my own life. For being the kind of friend who somehow magically draws out those things I don't even know yet are true until I tell you and for modeling a life of deep meaning and relationships and courage, I am grateful.

To my coaching clients. Thank you for your courage, your thoughtful questions, your vulnerability and your willingness to jump in the deep end. I am so honored to hold space for you and to support you in creating lives that you love. I know that our world is better off because you are in it. Watching you show up with ever more boldness, truth, and resiliency in your own work and lives is one of my very favorite things. Thank you for trusting me with your tears and laughter and for sharing your growth.

To Suzanne Stabile, Terry Saracino, Marion Gilbert and Renee Rosario, thank you for being such skillful Enneagram teachers and guides. You have opened this tool for me in ways that have changed my life and watching you hold space for transformational work in both large and small groups is incredibly inspiring. Marion, your work on the Enneagram and somatics has opened a new relationship for me with my own heart and body and continues to be one of the areas of the Enneagram that most fascinate me.

Terry, thank you especially for helping me gain permission to use the valuable descriptions of each type from the Enneagram Worldwide community in my chapter on the Enneagram. (See these descriptions and more at www.enneagramworldwide.com.) I am so grateful for the work of The Narrative Enneagram community and its mission to transform lives and create a more compassionate world.

To Zoë. Thank you for being the kind of friend who can sing to me when I have a crick in my neck and don't know how I'm going to hold it all together. I am still sad that I don't get to see you all the time since I had the audacity to move. But I love watching you bring your beautiful voice into the world. You inspire me.

To Erin, Caroline, and Sarah3. I am forever grateful for your wisdom and spiritual insights. And for your willingness to take my SOS texts regarding creativity cave meltdowns and respond with such TRUTH, compassion and powerful insights, as you always do. To Hannah, for being a source of inspiration and a space where I can always come to talk about The Really Real. I am so glad I found you all at Harvard Divinity School. You are my flock and you make me feel normal.

Katie and Denise, I look back over the last few years and am so grateful for your friendship, honesty and coaching prowess. I have deepened so much within these Martha Beck coaching tools because of the opportunity to learn with you. You are the definition of authentic, you know all the corners and crannies of my mind where I get lost and it has been one of my absolute favorite things to watch you all shine your healing art into the world. Keep it coming!

To Denise, everyone should have a spiritually wise friend like you who also happens to speak Enneagram. How many times have you helped me slow down, celebrate and go gentle with myself? I think the last time was like five minute ago when I texted you freaking out about finishing the final two chapters. You help me to wake up to the habits of my type and to make a fresh choice. This is some of the very best medicine and I am grateful.

To Skyler, thank you for holding my hand through the birth of this book. First of all, your gorgeous hashtag #showupmakemarks has completely made its way into my writer's and Instagram lexicons. You do show up and make marks and, when I am whipped by the creative process, I take comfort in the ways that you have walked before me. Late nights in the studio, stretching to take advanced encaustic painting courses before you thought you were ready (which now you are, ahem, teaching) and otherwise making art on your canvasses and out of your life. You are a soul sister in every sense. Thank you.

To Gretchen, for being such a skillful yoga teacher and inspiring friend. The way you have approached Iyengar yoga and shared your passion and skill has shifted my relationship to my body for the better and deepened my daily practice. Thank you.

To Cindy, for always asking the good questions. And for being a wise Three with a Four wing I can turn to when I can't see the way out of my own box.

To Parker, for writing books that helped stir in me a desire to live a more soulful and integrated life. And thank you for being a super lively conversation partner and Enneagram learner.

And to my dad, Jerry Pinkerton, for the generous and noble way that you move through the world and the countless opportunities you opened for me to travel, to study and to stretch. Thank you for always supporting me and believing in me. And to my sisters Heather and Jenae, thank you for loving me when I'm at my best and when I'm not and for honestly not seeming to even notice the difference. I love you both and am so grateful for your support, encouragement and love. And to Granny, for teaching me how to garden even when I was a kid and I pretended not to care. Your bougainvillea has been blooming over my shoulder the whole time I wrote this book. Thank you.

And to my mom Judy Pinkerton, thank you for helping take care of my children so I could write. Without those critical Saturdays I do not think this book would have gotten done in time. And for always reminding me that you love me for who I am, not what I do.

ABOUT THE AUTHOR

Courtney Pinkerton, M.Div & M.PP is a certified holistic life coach and the founder of Bird in Hand Coaching. She has helped hundreds of women wake up from the fog of busyness to contribute their most dynamic professional and creative gifts *and* enjoy their personal lives. She holds dual master's degrees from Harvard Divinity School and Harvard Kennedy School and is the creator of the eight-step Flourish Formula Coaching Program. Courtney holds a coaching certificate from Martha Beck International and teaches regular international retreats for women.

Website: courtneypinkerton.com
Email: cp@courtneypinkerton.com
Facebook: CourtneyPinkertonCoach
Instagram: courtneypinkerton

NOTES

NOTES

NOTES

NOTES

NOTES

NOTES

NOTES

THE FLOURISH KIT

The Flourish Kit is a collection of additional resources I have curated for readers of *The Flourish Formula*, to help you integrate these eight steps into your life to create lasting change.

**You can access the Free Flourish Kit at:
www.courtneypinkerton.com/flourishkit**

The kit includes:
- Your Self-Guided Retreat Planner
- Enneagram Quiz & Guide
- Video on Tapping: The Acupressure Points & How to Get Started
- Guided Meditation to Dissolve Your Stress
- Guided Meditation to Deal with Envy of Other's Accomplishments (*Mudita*)
- Ten Favorite Essential Oils & How to Use Them
- The Flourish Calendar Template

CPSIA information can be obtained
at www.ICGtesting.com
Printed in the USA
LVHW041809270920
667207LV00005B/1533

9 780999 409213